LEADING WHEN GOD Is Moving

Wayne Schmidt

Leading When God is Moving

Quantity discounts for group study:

1 - 9	$9.95
10-99	$7.95
99+	$5.95

To order, call
Wesleyan Publishing House

800-4 WESLEY

800-493-7539

Fax 800-788-3535

Copyright © 1996 by Wesleyan Publishing House
All Rights Reserved
Published by Wesleyan Publishing House
Indianapolis, Indiana 46250
Printed in the United States of America
ISBN 0-89827-166-5

First Printing June 1996
Second Printing December 1996

Scripture quotations marked (NIV) are taken from the HOLY BIBLE, NEW INTERNATIONAL VERSION®. NIV®. Copyright © 1973, 1978, 1984 by International Bible Society. Used by permission of Zondervan Publishing House. All rights reserved.

Scripture quotations marked (RSV) are taken from the Revised Standard Version of the Bible, copyrighted 1946, 1952, © 1971, 1973.

Scripture quotations marked (KJV) are taken from the Holy Bible, King James Version.

Table of Contents

9.95

98348

Introduction

Have you ever talked with someone and through that conversation sensed you were in the very presence of God? Several years ago I had the privilege, along with several other Wesleyan pastors, of spending a couple of hours with Dr. Adrian Rogers. We met in his spacious office at the Bellevue Baptist Church of Memphis, a historic Southern Baptist church with over 20,000 members and an annual budget in the multiple millions of dollars. It was easy to be awestruck simply by the atmosphere of the place.

But Dr. Rogers was even more impressive. With a humble spirit and resounding bass voice this genteel Southern gentleman generously shared his time and insights with us. His words were laden with the wisdom of personal experience and laced with scriptural references. He seemed to capture foundational truths in easy-to-remember phrases. The one that most impressed me that day was: "You can't spiritualize management issues and you can't manage spiritual issues."

His statement reveals a balancing act between two indispensable realities. First of all, there is no substitute for managing the ministry of a church professionally and thoughtfully. No amount of prayer or Bible study will replace the need to make even the toughest organizational decisions with integrity and good business sense. A spirit of revival will not neutralize the effects of poor financial management. Many spiritual leaders use the phrase "the church is different from other institutions" to justify sloppy administration. "You can't spiritualize management issues."

That is balanced, however, by a second axiom. No amount of organizational efficiency will bring about a movement of God's Spirit. Many churches are fiscally sound but spiritually dead. Some churches have committee structures that lead to carefully reviewed decisions, but leave no place for prayerfully seeking God's will for the church's future. If it doesn't fit on their organizational charts, God isn't allowed to do it! Spiritual life and revival are by-products of humbly seeking God. "You can't manage spiritual issues."

A movement of God is stimulated by recognizing leadership

principles while earnestly pursuing God's presence and purpose. As a spiritual leader, you cannot create a movement of God's Spirit . . . nor can you control it. But you can build an atmosphere conducive to spiritual momentum, thereby serving as a human catalyst for what God has decided to do. God has His part in a spiritual movement, and only He can do that part. You have your part in a spiritual movement, and God expects you to do it. Leaders must constantly discern both God's part and their part.

During the years I have had the privilege of serving as a pastor at Kentwood Community Church, God has richly blessed our congregation. The spiritual leaders of our church humbly recognize that much of the growth we've experienced is caused by the wind of the Spirit blowing across West Michigan. This sovereign choice by God has caused ministry expansion in numerous churches throughout our area. But we also recognize certain principles, reflecting sound management and consistent with Scripture, that we have followed. Our willingness to "do our part" has led our church to blossom while many surrounding churches are dying a slow and painful death. We are in the middle of a movement of God, and we are seeking as leaders to be faithful stewards of the opportunities provided by this moment in redemptive history.

The most incredible challenge has been managing change. Momentum requires people and programs to change. Change is relentless and a constant companion. There are changes God's Spirit initiates, and the failure to accept them results in being left behind in a movement of God. There are changes that are cultural, and we must be able to read them and then redeem them. Spiritual leaders are change managers.

Change can be intimidating, but it can also create new openness in the hearts and minds of people. It has a potentially destructive streak and can cripple a church. However, a victim mentality is not the mind-set of the spiritual leaders God is using in His church today. Change calls for new commitments, and God has always delighted in responding to the courageous commitments of His people.

The Old Testament book of Joshua is loaded with spiritual principles for change leadership. At first glance, it appears to be only a book about battles. That's the way leading people through change sometimes feels — one battle after another! We may be surprised that Joshua, in the process of pursuing God's plan, encounters so much opposition. It reminds us that even the highest of callings will include some testing along the way.

We're going to follow Joshua's footsteps, witnessing the evidence of

God at work and learning some of God's expectations for spiritual leaders. We'll also observe how momentum in a movement of God is developed through the proper management of change. The first four chapters of Joshua will expose some common myths that cause confusion among many sincere people who are seeking to faithfully lead in a local church. Here's just a sampler:

Myth #1 - "A church's history flows uninterrupted and smooth transitions are to be expected."

In reality, the history of a church is like a book. There are certain defining moments when one chapter in a church's life closes and another opens. These can be times of uncertainty as well as opportunity.

Myth #2 - "If something is God's will, everyone will feel good about it."

No, even changes that honor God result in a feeling of loss or resistance. People need time to adjust to even those initiatives which are born in the heart of God.

Myth #3 - "You can do it all."

Wrong. Even the largest churches do not have the resources to excel in meeting every need a community of people might experience. Vision must be brought into focus and priorities for ministry established.

Myth #4 - "Leadership is easy in a church that's experiencing a movement of God."

That's wishful thinking. Visionary leadership will call for tremendous courage and character. A church that is moving forward requires its leaders to constantly exercise faith as they invest their personal credibility to encourage commitment in the lives of others.

Myth #5 - "Great churches are built around a great leader."

Not in the long run. It is true that a God-given vision is often birthed in the heart of one person, and that person gets the ball rolling. But a lone ranger approach to ministry that is centered on the performance of one individual will have little lasting impact.

Myth #6 - "Great faith ignores the obstacles."

No. Great faith is accompanied by wisdom, and wisdom carefully assesses the obstacles as well as the opportunities.

Faith is not limited by challenges, but it is informed by recognizing those challenges.

Myth #7 - "You can't be too careful."

Yes you can! Many churches wait for the perfect conditions to move forward, and there is little perfect this side of heaven. The "paralysis of analysis" has been the Achilles' heel of many churches that fail to move forward with God's plan.

Myth #8 - "Success is elusive and temporary."

In reality, when the pursuit of success is focused upon God and honors Him, there can be a lasting legacy that blesses subsequent generations and the surrounding community for years to come. The results can be eternal!

I must confess that these myths arise not only out of the book of Joshua, but also out of my life. As a pastor, I have at times succumbed to belief in each of them. When I did, it hindered God's work in my life and ministry. Growing churches develop convictions around truths evident in God's Word. Decaying churches embrace misconceptions arising from myths like those mentioned above.

Momentum in ministry is a sacred trust. Spiritual leaders have the responsibility to sense where God is leading and to mobilize His people to follow. Our journey through Joshua will unveil leadership practices which both fuel momentum and frustrate it. The principles we will discover work in a church of any size and of any age, though in some settings it is harder work than others! Each chapter begins with a contrast between those commitments which help momentum and those which hinder it.

I've written this book with a variety of possible uses in mind. First of all, a leader might use it for personal Bible study and leadership training. Whether you are a pastor or lay person, an awareness of what contributed to Joshua's effectiveness will yield fruit in both your life and your ministry. It strikes me that Joshua reads a bit like a journal, as if he noted his observations in a diary while he lived them in everyday life. Imagine yourself as you read these pages looking over Joshua's shoulder and into his journal. You may want to keep a journal of your own, noting observations for the situation in which God has placed you.

Second, it can be used for discipling leaders in ministry management. So often the forward progress of a church is hamstrung by the leaders' insufficient grasp of the dynamics of change and inability to capitalize on those dynamics. This book might be utilized as a study guide for church staffs, boards or task forces as they pursue a clearer understanding of what is required to lay hold of the future God has prepared for them.

Third, it might be the basis of a series of sermons, or small group and Sunday School lessons. When I shared the material found in this book during our Sunday morning services, I applied it to an individual pursuing his or her God-given purpose as well as to the life of our church. Because so many people are dealing with change in their families, workplaces and communities, the truths here resonate with the dilemmas faced in day-to-day living.

Each chapter concludes with some follow-up material to help the book serve in the above-mentioned ways. My prayer is that it will be so much more than words on a page providing food for thought. Like Joshua, we need a new generation of leadership to prompt God's people to act upon God's promises. We need you.

Momentum is developed by recognizing the need for a new beginning and seeking what God will do next.

Momentum is drained by denying the need for change and continuing to live in the past.

Chapter One

Where Do We Go From Here?

"Those with the greatest vested interest in the present paradigm are least likely to see the new paradigm."

Joel Barker, *Future Edge*[1]

Joshua's Journal 1:1-2

"Forget the former things; do not dwell on the past. See, I am doing a new thing! Now it springs up; do you not perceive it?" (Isaiah 43:18-19a)

Imagine yourself as an unchurched person. You're driving through a community looking for a church. That nagging void in your life is longing for fulfillment and, after trying almost everything else, you decide to visit a church. Going with a friend might obligate you to continue, so you decide to drop in anonymously.

You locate a church near your neighborhood. You're a little concerned because it appears "stuck in time." The last coat of paint and the last additions to the landscaping appear to be nearly as old as the broken down bus parked behind the church. Your guess is that the church was built sometime in the 1950s, and the last real care it received took place in the 1970s. Unlike most, you decide you'll risk a visit.

You cautiously enter the facility. You have no idea where the restrooms are, so you assume the wind didn't adversely affect your hair. You're grateful you didn't bring the kids because a passing glance at the nursery gives you suspicions about whether it's safe and clean. Your search of the literature rack is fruitless; the old Sunday school literature and issue-oriented newsletters are probably meaningful to the members, but answer few of your most basic questions about this local church.

You sense the people there love God and know each other well. A few speak to you, but most huddle with their friends. The service begins with music unfamiliar to you but the singing is enthusiastic. The pastor asks if there are visitors, and you squirm in your seat as you feel you may be put on the spot. Fortunately, he appears not to see you (though you suspect you're the only visitor in the place). The message is presented with zeal, and while the pastor appears to be against a lot of things, he doesn't seem quite sure what to do about anything, or what the congregation should do. He uses some old phrases you haven't heard since your English literature class in college and quotes people you've never heard of. You're impressed with his sincerity, but have a hard time relating to him. You feel his everyday life is probably very different from yours and he would not understand the struggles you're facing.

You're relieved as you depart. Maybe those people have what you are looking for, and maybe you'll visit again. But you're going to try a few other churches first — something a bit more in your "time zone."

One of the greatest challenges spiritual leaders face is keeping in step with what God is doing today and where He is leading in the future. In the words of Isaiah, dwelling in the past blocks our vision of the new things God is seeking to do (43:18-19). If the past has been wonderful, you can celebrate it and thank God for it. If the past has been abysmal, you can lament it and hope for something better. You can rejoice because of it or grieve over it, but there's one option God never gives you — you can never live in the past.

I've been a pastor less than two decades. I've watched with interest the ministries of pastors who are ahead of me a few years, seeking to learn from their experiences. Some of them start brilliantly but reach the peak of their effectiveness early, then begin the long coast to retirement. Others begin uneventfully but are always looking for learning opportunities to keep them growing as persons and pastors. Their ministries gather strength as the years go by and the best days are still ahead. They are not "stuck in a rut," lacking purpose and direction.

As the book of Joshua opens we find a spiritual leader at the threshold of significant change. God is about to open a new chapter in the story of His people. Joshua's ability to provide leadership in this "new thing" God is doing depends on his willingness to perceive the transition God is bringing about.

Reading the Signals

A close examination of the first two verses of Joshua reveals more than a historical update. God is signaling to His chosen leader that the way things have been in the past will not continue into the future. The first is a change of leadership. The second is a change of location.

"Moses is dead." That legendary spiritual giant who guided God's people for so many years had gone the way of all mankind. God is doing more than stating the obvious — He is signaling a transition. Moses is dead . . . new leadership needs to emerge . . . and Joshua, you're that leader!

"Cross the Jordan River." No more wandering in the desert. The Promised Land that has been only a dream is about to become a reality. It's time to move out.

These are so much more than events — they signal the new thing God is about to do. Spiritual leaders have the ability to see the hand of God in the happenings of life. Perceiving the signals requires not only a watchful eye on circumstances, but a knowledge of Scripture.

Throughout Scripture a change in leadership is often the indicator of a new beginning. Sometimes that means raising up new leaders — Abraham to become the father of a great nation, Joseph to rescue God's people from famine, a prophet to proclaim God's warning to His people, Paul to spread the gospel throughout the world. At other times God replaces leadership — David steps into King Saul's position, Solomon assumes the throne of his father, Samuel replaces Eli.

Now "Moses is dead." God had said Moses would not enter the Promised Land, so the death of this great leader clears the way for the next movement of God. This signal is amplified by the command to prepare to "cross the river." Scriptural accounts of crossing water are often geographical thresholds of change and commitment in a movement of God. The miraculous crossing of the Red Sea when exiting Egypt would be impressed in the mind of every Hebrew, including Joshua. Now it's time to cross another body of water — the Jordan River.

Personal and spiritual growth depends on our ability to see one chapter of our life closing and a new one opening. These signals of transition come in different forms — a career change, the loss of a relationship, a physical move, health issues. They are met with either a desperate attempt to preserve the way things have been, or the recognition that things neither can nor ever will be the same.

What is true for you personally is also true for churches. The ability to perceive the new things God is doing keeps a movement of God fresh and vital. Ignorance or rejection of the signals relegates the best days of a church to the past. What are some of the common signals in the life of a church that things will never be the same?

Pastoral Change

Like Moses passing the baton to Joshua, so a new chapter in a church's history begins when God provides a new leader. I remember some years ago being contacted by a church asking if I might be interested in serving as their pastor. The church was still fairly young and the founding pastor was leaving. The lay leader who called me said, "We've benefited from the leadership of a Moses. Now we're looking for a Joshua to lead us in the next steps of obedience to the mission God has given us." While I did not accept their invitation, that was a transition signal even I couldn't miss!

Not all pastoral changes are made with a desire to embrace the future. Some pastoral selections are a reaction to a pastor who tried to implement change, so the church looks for someone who won't threaten the status quo. Or the previous pastor had certain strengths and, like all humans, corresponding weaknesses (the pastor who has only strengths and no weaknesses is a myth). The new pastor is selected with assets that are perceived to replace his predecessor's deficits. Whatever the motivation, a transition is under way.

I've served as a pastor at our church from its beginning. We started in a unique but effective way — I was the full-time assistant pastor while Dick Wynn, employed as well by Youth For Christ, served as the part-time senior pastor. I'll never forget the day Dick called me into his office to announce that he was accepting a promotion with Youth For Christ and would be moving to their national offices in Wheaton, Ill. I felt a hollowness in the pit of my stomach as I considered the absence of this man who had been my mentor and had led our church for the first two years of its history (1979 - 1981). My "Moses" wasn't dead, but he was moving out of town!

I had just celebrated my 24th birthday, and now was being asked to become what was somewhat humorously labeled the "senior" pastor. When it was publicly announced, most of the congregation was supportive but feeling the same nervousness I felt. I'll never forget one reaction, though. A man in our congregation who had served previously as a pastor told me that he and his wife would be leaving. His explanation? With Dick gone and me as the pastor, they didn't see the church surviving! Now there's a confidence booster!

A pastoral change brings about transition. Some in the church will view it positively, some negatively. It is doubtful that all will view it the same way.

Facility Changes

Our church began in rented facilities. After four months, we moved to a school that we also rented. After another three-and-a-half years, we finally moved into a facility we had built ourselves and which had a mortgage with our name on it. We were not prepared for what happened next.

We had struggled for nearly four years to assemble a core group for the church. Rented facilities brought numerous inconveniences — from the lack of classrooms to the lack of control over heat and air conditioning. Almost everyone there believed in the mission and the future of the church; they certainly weren't attracted by the facilities or extensive programs!

Then we opened the door of the church we had just built. People came . . . and came . . . and came. Our attendance doubled in one Sunday! These people didn't know what we believed. We'd made no major changes in our staff or approach to ministry. The only difference was that the facility they had watched being constructed was now completed. Then we learned that in our community, facility equaled credibility. They now took us seriously. We were a "real" church. Their perception of us had changed, and our church would never be the same.

Change of Lay Leadership

In so many churches across America, the long-term stability of a congregation is more dependent upon a lay leader or a small group of lay leaders than on the pastor. Sometimes this stability leads to church health. At other times it lends to the preservation of the status quo, whether that is healthy or not. In these churches a change in lay leadership can signal the closing of one chapter and the opening of the next.

This is particularly true in smaller, more rural churches. If a lay leader dies, or relocates due to retirement or a job transfer, the church experiences a period of adjustment. It is also true, though perhaps to a lesser extent, in larger churches. We have a voluntary rotation system for our board members. The general practice is to serve up to three years and then take at least a year off. Depending on who is rotating off (or on), this change can bring about a new emphasis or direction.

Breaking Through Growth Barriers

As a church grows, it not only becomes larger but it fundamentally changes. Resistance to these changes by the pastor or the people is the reason most churches finally plateau. Many of these growth barriers or thresholds have been identified by researchers like Carl George, author of the book *How To Break The Growth Barriers*.[2] There are certain predictable transitions that come as a church enlarges numerically.

Like most pastors, one of the toughest transitions for me was the "200" barrier. During the first four years of our church's existence, I knew almost everyone and everyone knew me. I had coffee in their homes, could name their kids, knew where they worked and the hobbies they enjoyed. Then we moved into our new church, experienced an influx of new people, and I found myself speaking to a sea of unrecognizable faces. While I was on cloud nine because of the outreach taking place, I struggled with my inability to personally minister to everyone.

While this was a secret struggle, on one occasion I shared my feelings with a dear older saint in our church. As I sat in her home enjoying one of her delicious homemade cookies, I bemoaned the fact I couldn't visit with everyone who was coming in. She very lovingly assured me that she and others would miss those fairly frequent visits as well. Then she said something I'll never forget: "Wayne, we love you and it's good to get to know you. But it's just more important that people get to know Jesus than get to know you."

The Holy Spirit brought those words home to my heart with conviction. Would I limit what God was doing to my personal comfort zones, or would I adjust my comfort zones to be in step with Him? That day I made a commitment I've needed to revisit many times since — that "bearing my cross" means obeying God even if

16

it's uncomfortable.

In *Growing Plans*, Lyle Schaller identifies and illustrates how a church changes as it grows.[3] He makes clear what so many church leaders have learned — a growing church is a changing church. A large church is not an overgrown small church. Its life is governed by a fundamentally different set of principles.

Community Changes

Not only do churches change, but communities do as well. If a major employer moves out of a community (or moves in), a church is impacted. If the ethnic or economic demographics of a community change, the effectiveness of a church's outreach is altered. If a rural community is absorbed in the urban sprawl of a metropolitan area, expectations for a church's ministry change.

Our church is committed to parenting new churches. We particularly target outlying communities in the greater Grand Rapids area. These communities are not only growing as Grand Rapids does, but they are changing. The people moving in are no longer farmers, but commuters who work in the city. The churches that have traditionally existed in the communities continue to be effective in ministering to long-term residents, but struggle to meet the needs of the changing population. These new residents have different social and spiritual needs. Often a new church best meets those needs, but many existing churches are learning to broaden their ministries to include a wider variety of people.

These are but a few of the transition times churches are facing. Some transitions are the result of conscious decisions a church has made — such as offering multiple services, adjusting worship styles, or providing pastoral care through small groups. Others are the result of factors beyond the control of church leaders. Like Joshua, they must adjust to the realities of external conditions over which they exercise little control.

Sensing the Loss

There is a myth that keeps many people from changing and many spiritual leaders from taking action when God's Spirit prompts them. The myth is this: "If it is God's will, everyone will feel good about it." In reality, the first feeling that comes with most substantive transitions is a sense of loss and a tendency to resist that change. In fact, scholars who study change dynamics have concluded that if there is no sense of loss and there is no resistance, there has been no real change!

So every change involves a sense of loss, even when we are excited about it. When a chapter in a person's life or a local church closes, a grief process takes place. If we could peer into Joshua's Journal, I'm convinced he would be experiencing the whirlwind of emotions that comes with "letting go" of the past.

Loss of Identity

Joshua had been known for years as "Moses' aide." Now Moses was dead. Joshua's relationship with Moses had given him his identity. Like many men, what defined him included the role he held. For years people had undoubtedly pointed him out with the words, "There's Joshua, Moses' assistant."

His relationship with Moses was much more than formal. Moses had been his spiritual director and mentor. They had shared many significant spiritual moments together:

- They had fought battles together. Joshua had wielded a sword in physical battle while he saw Moses with hands lifted high carrying on the spiritual battle (Exodus 17:8-16). Undoubtedly that day he learned that the future battles he fought would be so much more than struggles with flesh and blood — they would require prayer and dependence on God.
- Joshua had been trusted by Moses with a special assignment to spy out the Promised Land (Numbers 13-14). Joshua along with Caleb had encouraged Moses and the people of Israel with the challenge that they could take the land.
- Joshua had defended Moses' right to lead the people and speak for God (Numbers 11:26-30). Moses had taught him that not all spiritual authority and blessings were confined to the leader God had chosen.
- Joshua was present during many of Moses' intimate encounters with God (Exodus 33-34).

Joshua was an aide to a great spiritual leader. No one was nor would ever be like Moses, even in God's eyes (Deuteronomy 34:10-12). Joshua would never again be able to ask him questions, watch his actions or seek his prayers. Moses was dead.

A friend once shared with me his difficulty in adjusting to the death of his father. His sense of loss was amplified when he called his father's home not long after the funeral. With all the activity that had taken place, no one had thought to change the message on the answering machine. So he heard his father's voice saying, "I'm not available to take your call right now." He realized in that moment that his dad would never "be available" to take his calls. An incredible feeling of loneliness and loss overtook him. Joshua must have felt the same. Moses was no longer personally available to respond to him.

Loss of Familiarity

"Now then . . . cross the Jordan River into the land I am about to give to them — the Israelites" (Joshua 1:2). They were about to fulfill the dream God had given them decades previously. But they were also leaving the only way of life they had ever known. This generation had grown up in the desert. They were familiar with the ways of the desert, while that which was yet to come would be new territory.

Think of the "maintenance mentality" that developed during those desert wanderings. Having no hope for the future, their parents must have continually shared stories about "the good 'ol days." Undoubtedly the story of the ten plagues and the crossing of the Red Sea were fireside favorites! They heard the stories of a movement of God, but this new generation had never experienced a movement of God first-hand. They had a second-hand faith and forty years in the maintenance mode while God disposed of their unfaithful forefathers.

Adopting a "consumer mentality," their lives centered around their own needs. They approached God with a "feed me" mentality, expecting manna from heaven and then complaining about it when it arrived. When their needs were not met, their consumerism led them to whine to each other and question the authority of their leaders . . . even the great Moses.

Stuck in a rut and focused on their own needs. That description is fitting for more than half the churches in existence today! For the Israelites, their circumstances were familiar and therefore comfortable. Now Joshua had to lead them into unfamiliar territory. They wanted guarantees he couldn't give. They wanted to know exactly what this new land was like, how they would get their food, what would be expected of them. These were questions he could not completely answer, since he had only briefly visited this territory decades earlier. He wasn't familiar with the challenges they would face in that land today. They could only meet them as they faced them. They would have to exercise faith which, by definition, means moving beyond the familiar.

It's precisely at this point that many churches experience what Robert Dale labels "nostalgia" or "organizational homesickness." In his book *To Dream Again*, he observes that the word "nostalgia" is derived from two

Greek words meaning "to return home" and "a painful condition."[4] Change can prompt wistful longings in all of us. When movements of God are between chapters, the future can seem threatening and the past attractive. This causes some tentativeness. As a temporary condition, it is fairly harmless and normal.

The loss of the familiar, even when the familiar is a result of disobedience to God, is still a loss. I've been with families who wanted to structure an "intervention" to confront an alcoholic family member. Their sincere desire was to see a change in that person. I've also watched those same families undercut that person's attempt to change when they recognized their lives would be different as well. The present was dysfunctional, even sinful, but it was familiar.

All that was happening to Joshua and Israel was God's will, but taking hold of the future would mean letting go of the past. There's a certain amount of grieving that's normal anytime God brings about change in the life of a person or a church. The process looks like this:

Step 1 Denial. The focus is on the past. Nothing needs to change. Problems will go away. Effort is given to preserve things as they have been.

Step 2 Discomfort. There are changes taking place. Things will never be the same. Resistance to these changes and anger about them are typical reactions.

Step 3 Discovery. There is a willingness to begin to explore the future. The next step is unclear and unfamiliar, but possible opportunities begin to emerge.

Step 4 Devotion. Commitment emerges to act upon a new vision of the future.

Spiritual leaders realize that change, even when it's God's will, is a process. Not everyone may feel good about it. Many times our first reaction to God's conviction is one of denial and discomfort. He persists in the process until we adjust to His plans for us.

Leaders need to show the same kind of persistence. If people react hesitantly to a future vision, is that a sign it's not of God? Not necessarily. Is it a sign the people aren't spiritual? Not necessarily. It's a sign that we're human and that change means the loss of the way things are in order to prepare for the way God wants them to be.

Preparing To Move On

"Now then, you and all these people, get ready . . ." (Joshua 1:2). As you're closing one chapter, begin preparing for the transition into the next chapter. Don't forget the lessons of the past, but prepare to move beyond past patterns and experiences.

This transition time would have been a "double-whammy" for Joshua. At the same time he was working through a loss, he needed to learn new skills. He was no longer the assistant but the leader. The people were no longer desert nomads but a conquering army. They had one foot in history while stepping with the other foot toward a new opportunity. One chapter rarely closes completely before the next starts to open. For a while transition means uncomfortably straddling chapters.

Preparing to move on with God is somewhat different for each person or church, but these guidelines may help you prepare for the transition:

• **Acknowledge the loss**

Anyone familiar with the grieving process knows that it varies for each person. It's impossible to predict the exact emotions a person will feel or the time it will take to work through them. But one thing is certain — you may resist the grieving process or welcome it, but you will go through it.

When making the transition from one chapter to the next, the degree of loss depends on how much the previous chapter was valued and how much excitement the next one holds. If someone has derived great value and pleasure from the previous chapter, the loss will be intense. If someone is glad to close that previous chapter so they can move into an intriguing and exciting next chapter, the sense of loss is minimized.

The challenge is that people tend to value "chapters" differently. Think for a moment of a married couple. The husband may find it very difficult to change chapters in his career — most men receive much of their identity from their careers. The wife, on the other hand, may find it very difficult to change chapters at home. He may not understand why an impending "empty nest" bothers her so much, while she may view his reaction to a change in job responsibilities as being too extreme. That's why times of transition call for increased communication and understanding in a marriage.

The same is true for a church. When we're finding it difficult to see eye-to-eye at our church, we talk about "not being on the same page." In reality, sometimes we are not in the same chapter! Church members often have an emotional investment in different "chapters" of a church's history. So potentially each member will react to change a little differently. Allowing people to grieve over the past so they can move into the future calls for increased communication and understanding, not impatience or avoidance of the issues.

• Process Change At Your Speed

How you process change is influenced by more than the sense of loss you experience. It is influenced by your personality. Some people gain a sense of security from the past while others are continually pursuing the next big challenge. Some latch on to the big picture and are invigorated by pursuing the unexplored, while others have an eye for detail and are interested only in the next step.

The speed of processing a change is also influenced by whether you believe you've had a choice in the change. Resistance is much greater when you feel a change has been forced upon you. The more you're part of the process of change and have had a voice in shaping the next chapter, the more ready you'll be to welcome what is coming next.

Another factor is your past experience with change. If you have had to make very few changes in your job or family situation, any change seems imposing because you've had little opportunity to manage change previously. On the other end of the continuum, if you feel your whole life is one change after another, you may feel overwhelmed and may long for one area of life to remain the same. Your "change overload" at work and home may lead you to defend "the way things are" at church so that you can have a "secure sanctuary" in a changing world.

The speed at which you process change is influenced by your sense of loss, your personality, your experiences and the power you feel you have over the process. The same is true for every person in a church. Understanding these differences will hopefully create some freedom for each person to make transitions at his or her own pace.

• Don't Get Stuck Between Chapters

While each of us has the right to process change at our own

speed, we do not have the right to stop the process. Any healthy grieving process ultimately involves moving beyond the sense of loss over "the way things were" and into active pursuit of the way God wants them to be.

Transition times tend to make or break individuals. Harbored anger or a root of bitterness causes us to miss out on God's grace (Hebrews 12:15). Prolonged "pity parties" drain a person of the strength and vision to pursue the future work God desires them to do in life. A choice must be made to move on. That choice may not be rooted in desire or personal fulfillment. It may come out of a sense of responsibility to our relationship with God and with others. Feelings need to be acknowledged but not enthroned. Joshua may have *felt* that Moses' death couldn't have come at a worse time — right when they needed to conquer enemy forces and acquire the Promised Land. But Joshua also knew that God expected him to "get ready to cross the Jordan river into the land I am about to give . . ." (1:2).

Transition times also make or break churches. So many churches are stuck between chapters, in the no-man's-land of dwelling in the past and hesitating about the future. The felt needs of the members carry greater weight than a commitment to obedience. God patiently allows churches to adjust to change, but He also expects spiritual leaders to prepare for the next chapter of His great redemptive story that is about to unfold.

• Watch Your Focus

Yes, Joshua, "Moses is dead." But God is alive and well! Resist the tendency to become absorbed in your own emotions or react to the feelings of others. A vertical focus is essential. Keep one eye on what is happening *to* you and the other eye on what God is doing *in* you.

Getting ready to move on what God is doing means listening to Him. It involves knowing not only what God has done (through His Word or your personal experiences), but what God will do for you and for His people in the days ahead.

Anticipating the Future

God begins his conversation with Joshua by looking back: "Moses is dead." He continues it by sharing with him what needs to take place now:

"Get ready." He's acknowledged past realities and defined the present action step; now He shifts the focus to the future. Prepare to enter "into the land I am about to give to them — to the Israelites." Start anticipating what is yet to come.

Anticipating the future does not mean rejecting the past, but learning from it so that you can move forward. Like rowing a boat, you face backwards only to more effectively move forward. You look back not because that is the direction you are intending to go, but because it maximizes your strength and gives you reference points in moving ahead.

One of the great joys God grants us is anticipation. Sometimes anticipation exceeds reality! Anticipating a vacation may be better than the vacation itself. Looking forward to retirement may be better than living in retirement. Dreaming about owning a business may be more hassle-free than being the actual owner.

The Christian life is one of anticipation. We look forward to God's answers to our prayers. We seek to discover His will for our lives, knowing that our stewardship of time, abilities and money has eternal consequence. By faith we believe all the injustices of human existence will eventually be addressed and that eternity will reveal the reward of faithful service to our Heavenly Father. We know the final reality of heaven will exceed any of our anticipation!

Anticipating our final destination may be easier than anticipating the next step God has for us as we journey with Him. Like Joshua, we know there will be thresholds of commitment to cross, battles to be waged and comfort zones to be stretched. God will do His part, but He expects us to obediently complete our part as well.

While transition begins with the loss experienced in "closing a chapter," it reaches its fruition in the anticipation of "opening a new chapter." These times of change create opportunities for greater dependence upon God and greater openness to His plan for us. Spiritual leaders and churches also need to welcome these chapter changes, anticipating the blessing of experiencing first-hand a participation in a movement of God.

Personal Reflection

1. How "up-to-date" is my relationship with God? When is the last time I obeyed God in a way that significantly stretched my faith?

2. As I evaluate my own personal history, what are some of the key transition moments I experienced? (Look for spiritual changes, relationships beginning or ending, career or geographical moves,

influential people or events, family transitions.)

3. How open do I see myself being to the changes God brings about in my life? In terms of God's timing, do I tend to move too quickly or too slowly?

4. As I assess the current status of my life, am I:
   • mourning the loss a significant change in my life has created?
   • stuck "between chapters"?
   • anticipating what God is going to do next in and through me?

5. Additional Reading: *Why You Do What You Do* by Bob Biehl.[5]

Inventory for Spiritual Leaders

1. Can you identify some of the "chapter transitions" in your local church's history? (It may help to review some of the transition signals highlighted in this chapter.)
   a. How was your church founded? By whom? Why? What were its founding values, and how appropriate are they for the present and future?
   b. What are the patterns of attendance, conversions and finances recorded in your statistical history?
   c. What are the notable events and frequently told stories? What years are considered the "golden years" by most members?

2. Where is your church in the change process:
   a. Denial — most see little need for change.
   b. Discomfort — there is resistance to making any substantive changes.
   c. Discovery — we're praying about and seeking God's will for our future.
   d. Devotion — the congregation is committed to a specific plan for moving forward.

3. What are ways you can lead your church to focus on God during times of transition?

4. Are you anticipating the future?
   a. What opportunities do you see for outreach in your community?
   b. What new ministries would you like to see initiated?
   c. What areas of growth must you experience to equip you to lead in a movement of God?

5. Additional Reading: *To Dream Again* by Robert Dale.

Joshua's Journal:

Lord, I've lost a trusted mentor and spiritual director. How I wish he were here as I face the greatest challenge of my life! Help me to trust in You. Help me to move in concert with Your will both for my internal development and for my spiritual leadership. Give me wisdom as I help Your people adjust from what has become so familiar to that which will stretch their faith. Help me to be patient as they say good-bye to the past, but persistent in helping them to look to the future. Amen.

FOOTNOTES

1. Barker, Joel Arthur, *Future Edge* (New York: William Morrow and Co., 1992), paraphrase of pages 68-69.
2. Carl George, *How To Break The Growth Barriers* (Grand Rapids: Baker Books, 1993).
3. Lyle Schaller, *Growing Plans* (Nashville: Abingdon Press, 1983).
4. Robert Dale, *To Dream Again* (Nashville: Broadman Press, 1981), p. 107.
5. Bobb Biehl, *Why You Do What You Do* (Nashville: Thomas Nelson Publishers, 1993).

Momentum is developed by creating a clear and focused vision statement.
Momentum is drained by shooting at nothing
or attempting to do everything.

Chapter Two

Discovering God's New Frontier

"The place where God calls you is where your deep
gladness and the world's deep hunger intersect."[1]
Frederick Buechner

Joshua's Journal 1:3-5

"May He remember all your sacrifices and accept your burnt offerings. May
He give you the desire of your heart and make all your plans succeed"
(Psalm 20:3-4).

You see them every day at work, in your neighborhood, even at church.
People who drag through life, day in, day out, year after repetitive
year. People who are grinding away their lives and spending their time
on tasks that fail to challenge their souls. They seem sedated by the
monotony of a life that is too small for the "breath of God" that is within

them. Their spirits long for a movement of God to envelop their inner being and give them purpose for living.

Over time, apathy and negativism develop. In the words of Price Pritchett, "Unable to make any promising connection between a troubled today and a vague tomorrow, they fall into a weary pattern of doubt, cynicism, and disillusionment."[2] Maybe that's why we live in a society that places so little hope and trust in government, schools or the church. Maybe that's why God is raising up spiritual leaders who live their lives "on purpose" . . . and lead their churches to do the same.

Joshua knows that God is opening a new chapter in the life of His people. While sensing the loss of "the way things were," he knows he cannot back into the future. He must look forward to God's purpose for the days ahead. This purpose is pointedly revealed in Joshua 1:3-5. A closer look at these verses provides a lesson for spiritual leaders in the indispensable dimensions of a God-given vision.

Seek the Opportunities

The best opportunities are those which fulfill the promises of God. God tells Joshua, "I will give you every place where you set your foot, as I promised Moses. Your territory will extend . . ." (1:3-4). God is unveiling a glimpse of the opportunities that lie ahead in the movement underway. I can't help but notice that it's just God and Joshua, alone in conversation about the future God has prepared.

I am an avid reader of what is taking place in churches around our nation. I often visit churches that are a bit ahead of us in their development or in a particular area of ministry. I get on the phone with other pastors to ask them what they are doing. I survey our congregation and talk with our leadership teams. But I am convinced that apart from time alone with God all of those activities are futile. It is persistence in prayer that will move your church's ministry plan beyond mimicking what others are doing to fulfill God's unique promises to you.

You are created in the image of God. That gives you the ability to be creative, to see that which is unseen. You not only can sense the future, but have a role in creating it. This capacity is part of the created order, God's design for humanity. It even works apart from God! Many people with no allegiance to God accomplish great things through possibility thinking and visualization of the future. But God seeks to sanctify that creative capacity so that the possibilities envisioned are based on His promises and aligned with His purposes.

While it would be wonderful to think that vision is a characteristic most plentifully found among the people of God, many churches fail to seek God-promised opportunities. Joshua and the Israelites were not naturally inclined to envision the future because of the "blinders" they were wearing. Which of the blinders present in their lives then are found among churches today?

- **They had been wandering without a specific direction for a long time**. They had spent forty years as shepherds in the desert, marking the passage of time. It was the fulfillment of God's declaration to the previous generation, "Your children will be shepherds here for forty years . . . For forty years — one year for each of the forty days you explored the land — you will suffer for your sins and know what it is like to have me against you" (Numbers 14:33-34). The people whom Joshua would lead into the Promised Land had lived their whole lives meandering in a wasteland.

    Many churches have a history of wandering. They mark time by doing the same thing they have always done, not pursuing any specific direction. This makes it challenging to think clearly and specifically about future opportunities.

- **They had developed a "manna" mentality**. During their time in the desert, God miraculously provided their daily sustenance. Moses, their great leader, spent his time responding to their complaints about the menu. In their minds, leadership existed for the purpose of meeting their needs.

    Don't miss this blinder! Many Christians cannot envision anything beyond their own needs! There is a world of difference between believing that the purpose of leadership is to "meet my needs" and believing that the purpose of leadership is to "help us conquer new territory in obedience to God." God will not do great things through people whose only expectation of leadership is to "meet my needs." He can do great things through people who expect leaders to "conquer new territory." As a church ages, there is a tendency for the focus to move from reaching the community (taking new territory) to catering to the preferences of the members (meet my needs). Maybe that's why most churches reach their peak before they are two decades old.

    I've seen this tendency in our church . . . and in my life. When our church started, we *had* to "take new territory" for God. If we hadn't, we would not have survived. As time passed, it was so tempting to make our top priority meeting the needs of people who faithfully attended, served and gave. We began to judge the value of every worship service by "what we got out of it" instead of asking whether it was challenging to someone who did not yet know Christ. There is nothing wrong with having one's spiritual needs met. But there is a balance between meeting needs and taking new territory. A movement of God requires us to transcend self-centeredness to extend His kingdom.

- **What Joshua envisioned had been tried once and had failed**. Because of their unbelief, God had sentenced their forefathers to die in the desert. Unhappy with God's decision, they had taken matters into their own hands and tried to enter the Promised Land. ". . . in their presumption they went up toward the high hill country, though neither Moses nor the ark of the Lord's covenant moved from the camp. Then the Amalekites and Canaanites who lived in that hill country came down and attacked them and beat them down all the way to Hormah" (Numbers 14:44-45). Their defeat came as they belatedly tried to do what was no longer God's will. They attempted to conquer new territory in their own strength and without God's resources.

  So many times when a church begins to discuss future opportunities, we hear the words "that's been tried before, and it didn't work." It may be a reference to a past ministry initiative, fund-raising campaign or building program. A failure of the past limits opportunities for the future. The vision God was giving Joshua was no different from the one He'd given Moses: Enter the Promised Land. But a closer look reveals the most important difference of all — that this time the movement was God's will and He would provide the victory. Same task, but a new leader, new followers — and a renewed commitment from God.

- **They were suffering for the unfaithfulness of their forefathers**. Joshua had wandered in the desert for forty years, not because of his lack of vision or obedience, but because he was outvoted by ten other spies. The generation he was to lead into the Promised Land had not shared in the disobedient actions that brought about their desert experience. God had predicted it when He announced, "Your children will be shepherds here for forty years, *suffering for your unfaithfulness* . . ." (Numbers 14:33, italics added).

  It's tough when you have to suffer for your own sins. It's even tougher when you suffer because others have been unfaithful to God. I see it in the lives of individuals who have experienced abuse, been impacted by divorce or unjustly treated at work. There is a tremendous temptation to be bitter, which always magnifies the past and clouds the future. I have seen it in the lives of churches when past leaders did not take the necessary steps of faith. They become mired in the "should have beens" and "could have beens," completely missing what "yet could be" by the grace of God.

Courageous spiritual leaders won't allow the blinders of past experience to block their vision of God-given opportunities. In times of prayer, God reveals our blinders and challenges our self-centeredness or self-pity. He encourages us to step out and "take new territory" in our own spiritual lives and in the mission of our church. The experience of personal and public worship frees our desires to long for what God promises to provide. It is no mistake that when the Psalmist says, "May [the Lord] give you the desire of your heart and make all your plans succeed" (20:4), that the verse immediately preceding it says, "May He remember all your sacrifices and accept your burnt offerings" (20:3). Your worship (sacrifices) and self-denial (offerings) position you to seek the opportunities.

See the Boundaries

God promises Joshua, "I will give you every place where you set your foot . . ." But God also limits where Joshua will set his feet — the extent of the property. "Your territory will extend from the desert to Lebanon, and from the great river, the Euphrates — all the Hittite country — to the Great Sea on the west" (1:4). Those are the boundaries — the desert, Lebanon, Euphrates, the Great Sea.

A God-given vision includes not only the possibilities, but also the boundaries. We are created in the image of God, so we can sense the opportunities. Yet we are creatures, restricted by time and space. Like all creatures, there are limits to what can be done by one individual . . . or one church. Limits can be resisted, or they can be appreciated — but they are real.

I grew up in a small Wesleyan church. I remember hearing about large churches, though they were not common. I also remember pastors saying, "If we were a big church, we could . . ." Maybe that's why I came to believe that a big church could do it all. What a myth! I now have the responsibility of leading a church that would have fit my definition of "big" when I was growing up. Yet we're still struggling with the limitations of money, facility and personnel. A church never gets to the place where it can offer an endless "smorgasbord" of ministry opportunities — there will always be a need to set priorities and postpone some ministries to another day.

A clear vision statement includes not only what a church will say yes to, but what it will say no to as well. The ideal would be a statement clarified to the point that it could become a filter all church leaders could use with confidence. It would help them to say, "Yes, we'll be involved in that," but also to say, "While that ministry may be valuable, it doesn't fit within the territory God has promised to us."

Learning to say no is one of the toughest tasks of spiritual leaders. I remember as a young pastor hearing Dr. Orval Butcher say, "The problem with most Wesleyan churches is not who we are willing to win, but who we're not willing to lose." It was his way of saying he'd seen churches completely lose their vision and momentum in an attempt to appease one powerful person or interest group in the church. Attempts to please all the people or meet every need drain energy that might otherwise be focused on moving the vision forward.

Boundaries are like the banks of a river. Banks create depth and increase the momentum of the water as it flows. Rivers without banks are slow and shallow. Churches without boundaries in their vision statements try to please everyone, do everything and embrace the latest fad. The result is ministry that can be described as "a mile wide and an inch deep."

What makes it tough to say no is the tension it creates. Everybody gets excited about what can be done, but since Adam and Eve we've struggled with our creaturely limits. That struggle is intensified by living in a world that deceptively promises, "You can have it all." I've seen it in our church planting efforts. We bring in a church planter who begins to share his vision with a core group of people. This process is sometimes referred to as "agenda agreement." The core group may be excited to hear, for instance, that small groups will be a major emphasis in the life of that new church. "Pastoral" care will be given by the group leader and other members of the group. But what happens the first time one of those individuals is hospitalized and the small group leader visits but the pastor doesn't? Is pastoral care through small groups still a great idea? It is when something is *not* done that the implications of a vision become clear!

The church I serve graciously grants me a study break during the month of July each year. That "break" allows me to do advance work on sermon series, give prayerful and concentrated attention to refining our vision statement and ministry plan, and visit other churches on the weekends. A couple of years ago I visited several newer and smaller churches in our community. I was surprised by the number of people who had formerly attended our church and who were now part of these new churches. I sat in the back of one church and could identify by name 27 of the 63 people in the auditorium! I conducted some spontaneous "exit interviews," asking why they had chosen to leave our church. Several reasons were mentioned, but most often it was "that the church is just too big." I asked if they had been part of a small group or class, and most of them had not. But even those who had, expressed a desire to be part of a church where they recognized most of the faces in the worship services and could rather spontaneously spend time with the pastor. I left wanting to meet that need, but painfully recognizing I had encountered one of the "boundaries" of a larger church ministry. Large churches have limits. Small churches have limits. A clear vision acknowledges those limits.

Sometimes a vision dictates that the answer be, "No, it will never happen." As uncomfortable as it might be for me, our church will never be one big happy family. It's impossible to even get everyone in the sanctuary at the same time, let alone know everyone who is there! We are a church with lots of "families" — small groups, classes and special ministries. When we gather to worship, it is a family reunion — a gathering of "family" groups related by the blood of Christ.

At other times, the vision dictates, "No, we cannot do it at this time." We call this the principle of "uneven development." It's a myth to believe that a church develops its ministry simultaneously and equally on all fronts. I've witnessed this in our building programs. The first facility on our present site rather equally served the various ministry areas. Due to the rapid growth of attendance but a more limited growth in finances (why does it always seem to happen that way?), our next addition increased space for children's and youth ministries but did nothing to relieve overcrowding in worship. So we added additional services. When designing our new sanctuary, we addressed our needs for nurseries and worship space but had to postpone adding another educational wing and offices. We have told our congregation all along that no one building program will ever meet all our needs. Finances or facilities cause temporary limits. Sometimes those limits relate to time or to volunteers. The need fits within the framework of our vision, but not within our present resources.

Every time church leaders say yes (it's an opportunity) or no (it's a boundary), the vision becomes clearer. That's why vision statements must be "living," open to revision. The process of thinking through a vision is even more valuable than what ends up on paper. In the words of Peter Drucker, "Plans are nothing. Planning is everything." It's the exercise of listening to God, examining present realities and strategically considering the future that God uses to reveal His will to His people.

Set the Territories

When God promises Joshua to give him the land he walks on, it's obvious victory will come day by day, one step at a time. He'll not take all of the territory at once. He'll experience small successes on the way to embracing all that God has shown him. There would be territories within the Promised Land, eventually divided among the twelve tribes of Israel.

A spiritual leader establishes "territories" within his or her personal life mission statement. I'm convinced a spiritual leader should be accountable for goals in the various arenas of life. Among them are:

- Personal - maintaining a level of physical fitness, stretching my mind and opening my heart to share more of myself with others.

- Relational - allotting time and energy for my wife and my children, and deepening relationships so they develop beyond acquaintances to true friendships.

- Spiritual - exercising the spiritual disciplines of time spent in God's Word, prayer, Scripture memory, journaling and fasting.

- Vocational - honoring God with all of my work, whether paid or volunteer, constantly striving to produce lasting results.

- Financial - learning to be a good steward as I earn, give, save and enjoy what God has entrusted to me.

I find it helpful to periodically review the current priority each area holds in my life as evidenced in my actions, checkbook and calendar. I then recommit these "territories" to the desired priority level.

In a similar way, churches should identify "territories" in their vision statement of what God has promised them. In our vision statement, we call these "key result areas." Let me illustrate by sharing our current vision statement (subject to continual refinement). You'll notice there are three "stanzas" to it — one applying to our vision for ministry to current attenders (KCCers), one to the unchurched or "de-churched" around us (community), and the final one for missions (world):

For Every KCCer. . .
Activating steps of personal maturity in Christ within a large church family through holistic ministry.

For Our Community. . .
Initiating opportunities for every area home to experience the redemptive life of Christ through active church involvement.

For Our World. . .
Engaging in strategic regional, national and international outreach through partnership with other organizations.

Our vision statement is an attempt to succinctly express our strategy for impacting people for Christ. It does not stand alone, but is based on our mission statement. Our mission statement expresses the biblical foundation for our ministry:

To glorify God through active worship, empowering God's people for new levels of redemptive living and service, and building God's kingdom through thoughtful and creative communication of the changeless truth of Jesus Christ to a world that will never be the same.

Our mission statement is a brief synopsis of our theology of ministry; our vision statement is a brief synopsis of our strategy for ministry. Out of our vision come five "territories" of ministry, which we call our key result areas:

Relationship Networks
This first key result area expresses our commitment to help people care for one another by being in relationship with each other. It drives our attempts to multiply the number of our small groups and ensures there is a dimension of fellowship to our classes. As we acknowledge in our vision statement, we are a large church. We know that a sense of community will not be generated by knowing everyone. We teach our new members about four levels of fellowship:

Celebration: Worship times designed to help us fellowship with

God. These are intended to create intimacy with God but allow a level of anonymity with other people.

Connections: These are class settings that vary in size from 15-150. They are centered on instruction, but opportunity is provided to share names and prayer requests.

C.A.R.E.: Caring About Reaching Everyone is the theme of our small group ministry. Varying in size from 3-20, the goal is to share life experiences and build spiritual depth through caring for each other and praying for each other.

Covenant: These are one-on-one relationships (or groups of three) for the purpose of accountability. Meetings are based on a covenant to accomplish certain tangible goals to achieve personal and spiritual growth.

Relationship networks may begin during a worship time, but they will never develop there. It is in Connections, C.A.R.E. groups and Covenant partnerships that true fellowship is enriched.

Development of Personal Giftedness

Every believer is gifted by God for ministry. Lay ministers are most effective and most fulfilled when using their spiritual gifts in an area of service where they have a God-given passion.

Biblical Comprehension and Application

Alarmed by the level of biblical illiteracy present even among believers, we are committed to people discovering the "whole counsel of God" and applying it to their everyday lives.

Outreach to Area Homes

As expressed in our vision statement, we will take the initiative to introduce people to the redemptive life of Christ. We will not just passively wait for them to come to us, but actively build bridges to reach out to them. The focus of our strategy for evangelism is not on media or crusades, although we may utilize those means. It is to enfold people into the church.

Partnerships for Missions

We will partner with other organizations and people to most effectively reach our nation and world.

These five "territories" of ministry are reflected in the specific annual goals of every department of our church. Two things take place on a regular basis:

1. We monitor each key result area to ensure it is being lived out in the life of our church. If there is ever a time when one of these results is not being pursued, we are being unfaithful to our mission. By definition, a key result area is to be continually practiced and never neglected.

2. We rank these key result areas each year in order of priority. The one at the top of the list is our number one priority for that given year; the one on the bottom of the list is the lowest priority for that year. Again, all of them must take place each year, but the amount of attention given to each will vary from year to year depending on the opportunities that are present.

   For instance, as I write these words, we are in the process of building our new sanctuary. We hope to move into this facility about a year from now. At this present time, our number one key result area is "relationship networks." In this "Year of Small Groups," we are concentrating on building a strong fellowship base within our church. Our lowest key result area is "outreach to area homes," in part due to the limitations of our facilities. When we move into our new sanctuary, what will our number one key result area be? "Outreach to area homes." We will have a window of opportunity to make a significant impact on our community. We hope by that time to have developed relationship networks that will help newcomers sense the warmth of our fellowship.

   We tentatively project five years in advance the annual ranking of our key result areas. They are subject to change as we get closer to the actual year, but it does help us maintain a longer-term perspective on our shorter-term strategy.

Into what "territories" is God leading your church? What results are necessary for you to be faithful to the vision God is giving you?

Developing Your Vision For Ministry

If you've never attempted to create a written vision statement for your church, what I've shared with you may seem overwhelming and complex. Our vision statement has been generated over a period of years, and has enough detail to be sure all our staff and lay leaders are moving forward in the same direction. Your statement may be very different from ours, or it may closely resemble ours. The important thing is that it says what you sense God is saying to you.

Developing a vision is a process. In my life and in our church, the development of our original vision statement took place in this way:

1. I devoted considerable time to reading about vision. There are many excellent resources available from authors like Aubrey Malphurs, C. Peter Wagner, Bob Logan and George Barna. One of the briefest descriptions of the perspectives to be included in vision is penned by Bennis and Nanus in their book *Leaders*.[3] They highlight the following dimensions:

    Foresight: to judge how the vision fits with the way the environment of the organization may evolve.

    Hindsight: so that the vision does not violate the traditions and culture of the organization.

    World View: within which to determine the impact of possible new developments and trends.

    Depth Perception: so that the whole picture can be seen in appropriate detail and perspective.

    Peripheral Vision: so that possible responses of competitors and other stakeholders to the new direction can be comprehended.

    Revision: so that all visions previously synthesized are constantly reviewed as the environment changes.

    While these insights come from a secular book, I found it helpful to ask God for each of these dimensions of vision as I attempted to "see" our future.

2. I devoted concentrated time to prayer. I asked God to allow me to see things as He does and to know what new territory He wanted our church to conquer. During these times, I attempted to write a description of our church ten years from now, including people being reached, size, how lives were being changed, ministries that were being offered, facilities that had been built, etc.

3. I created a "rough draft" of our vision statement. Up to this point, the process of vision development had been just between God and me. Now I created something to which other leaders in our church could respond. Every copy was labeled "rough draft" to indicate the vision statement was in process and that other input would be welcome.

4. In meetings with our staff, church board and other lay leaders, we refined the vision statement. In most areas there was give and take, though in some areas I held firmly to the original draft. I found myself feeling a bit defensive since I had already spent so much time with the statement, but realized that the refinements suggested by others allowed for their ownership of the final statement.

5. It was presented to various groups within our church for their reaction and input. While by this time we were not making major revisions, their suggestions did serve to fine-tune our vision and expose some of the blind spots.

6. It was presented to the whole congregation for formal adoption. By this time nearly every leader in our church had seen it and been given an opportunity to respond to it, so the final adoption was more of a ceremonial event.

The first time we created a vision statement, the whole process took about ten months. Steps 1, 2 and 3 occurred rather simultaneously and took two to three months. Step 4 took an additional four months. Steps 5 and 6 took about three months. The length of the process depends on factors such as previous experience, the size of the church, the degree of unity among leaders, and the credibility of the pastor and church board. Remember, it is the process that's valuable, not just the final product. Don't rush it, but don't let it bog down. And every step of the way, listen to what God is promising you.

The Promises of God

A close look at Joshua 1:3-5 reveals that any vision from God involves more than the promise of results (1:3-4). It is centered on a relationship with Him (1:5). He promises Joshua that He will be with him every step of the way as the Israelites pursue the conquest of the Promised Land.

God never promises Joshua that it will be easy — in fact He talks to him next about the need for courage! He does not promise conflict-free conquest — there will be many battles and setbacks before Joshua's conquest is over. He does not promise an immediate conquest — it will take years for the territory to be taken.

He does promise results that are significant from God's perspective, and a relationship that will prove God is faithful and available every step of the way. God promises Joshua that he won't have to go it alone. No matter how challenging it becomes, God will be there.

Personal Reflection

1. Have I ever attempted to clarify my own personal life mission statement? For what purpose did God place me upon this earth?

2. Prayerfully consider these questions:
   a. Who have my role models been? What qualities do I admire in them?
   b. If I could be remembered for living by only one principle, what would it be?
   c. At the end of my life, if I could be remembered for only two accomplishments, what would they be?

3. In order to pursue my life vision, what must I say no to? What must I unlearn? Richard Bolles, in his book *What Color Is Your Parachute?,* recommends that we:
   a. **Unlearn** the idea that our mission is primarily to keep us busy doing something and **learn** that our mission is first to be the sons and daughters of God.
   b. **Unlearn** the idea that the unique and individual aspects of our mission are ordered by God without respect to our hearts and **learn** that God has created us to enjoy our mission.
   c. **Unlearn** the idea that our unique mission must be some achievement for all the world to see and **learn** instead that a stone does not always see the ripples it has caused.[4]

4. Establish the goals necessary to achieve my life mission and form an accountability partnership or group. It may be helpful to read *Accountability: Becoming People of Integrity.*[5]

Inventory for Spiritual Leaders

1. Review the "blinders" present among the people of God in Joshua's day that might have kept them from seeing the future. What blinders are present in your church?

2. What are some of the possibilities for ministry present in your church and your community? Think again (as you were challenged to do at the end of chapter one) about opportunities for outreach, new ministries that could be developed and necessary steps of growth for the people of your congregation.

3. What boundaries exist in your vision of ministry — what will you *not* do, at least in the near future? These include ministries already being done well by others that aren't essential to your vision and reflected in your gifts. For instance, at our church we've said no to:

a. Establishing a Christian school. We already have quite a few excellent Christian schools in our community.

b. Having our pastoral staff devote significant time to counseling. We have excellent counseling services nearby, and we cannot afford the investment of staff time.

You may choose to enter into these ministries, and others may choose to do the things you decide not to do. The important thing is that each church implements the ministries that fit the vision God has given them.

4. What are some of the "territories" or key result areas that your church should constantly pursue and monitor? Are they reflected in your vision statement?

Joshua's Journal:

Lord, it is an awesome mission that You have set before me. So much of it is hard to understand or envision from my current vantage point, but I vow to keep in step with You. While You've not promised easy or immediate accomplishment of this mission, You have promised to never leave me or forsake me. So I'll move courageously forward, for there is nothing that empowers a person more than Your promises and Your presence. Amen.

FOOTNOTES

1. Richard Nelson Bolles, *What Color Is Your Parachute?,* 1996 Edition (Berkeley: Ten Speed Press, 1996), p. 460.

2. Price Pritchett, *Firing Up Commitment During Organizational Change* (Dallas: Pritchett & Associates, 1994,) p. 5.

3. Warren G. Bennis and Burt Nanus, *Leaders: The Strategies For Taking Charge* (New York: Harper & Row, 1985).

4. Richard Nelson Bolles, *What Color Is Your Parachute?* 1995 Edition (Berkeley: Ten Speed Press, 1995).

5. Wayne Schmidt and Yvonne Prouwant, *Accountability: Becoming People of Integrity* (Indianapolis: Wesleyan Publishing House, 1991).

Momentum is developed through having the strength and courage to act upon God's will.

Momentum is drained by opting to remain in our comfort zones rather than following convictions.

Chapter Three

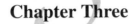

Courage That Counts

"Success is never final. Failure is never fatal. It is courage that counts."[1]
Winston Churchill

Joshua 1:6-9

"Be on your guard; stand firm in the faith; be men of courage; be strong" (1 Corinthians 16:13).

Imagine a blossoming courtship between a young man and a young woman. As their relationship begins, they are cautious about sharing too much of their hearts until they know one another better. As time goes on, they enjoy each other's company and begin to reveal more of themselves. They may even begin to look to the future, dreaming about what it would be like to spend the rest of their lives together.

Up to this point, their future has been a matter of conversation and imagination. If the relationship is to last, there will come a time when they ponder their commitment to each other. Will I give myself only to this person — "for better, for worse, for richer, for poorer, as long as we both shall live?"

The first few verses of Joshua allow us to eavesdrop on a conversation between God and His newly appointed leader. A movement of God begins with a person who is willing to listen to the purposes of a sovereign God for His people. Up to this point, everything that has been communicated has been just between God and Joshua.

That's about to change. Soon Joshua will "go public" and announce God's vision for the days ahead. He'll begin to challenge other leaders and prepare the people to move into the Promised Land. It's time for a "gut check" — an internal test to be certain Joshua has the commitment to pursue the vision, "for better, for worse, for richer, for poorer." Is the vision of God he has received simply a good idea, or will he obey God every step of the way until it becomes a reality?

In the days that lie just ahead there will be few tangible rewards for this new leader. The only thing that will keep the vision alive, from a human perspective, is the leader's faith and commitment. Getting this movement off the ground will require constant attention to problems not previously encountered. In a word, it will require **courage**. And that's exactly what God addresses in Joshua 1:6-9.

Courage For Influence

"Be strong and courageous, because you will *lead* these people . . ." (1:6, emphasis added). Joshua had been Moses' aide, but now he is the point person in a fresh movement of God. One doesn't need great courage to be influenced by others. One must be strong and courageous, however, if he or she intends to influence others.

God knows that if Joshua provides lukewarm leadership, this movement isn't going to make it into the Promised Land. There are many good ideas and great dreams. There are many people who hear God whisper His intentions for their lives. But without a passionate investment of energy and influence, they will never conquer new territory.

I'm convinced that spiritual leaders and churches that are growing aren't more creative than those which aren't growing. And they may not be more spiritual. What is the difference? It is the courage to act upon what God shows them — to be an influence rather than to simply respond to the random requests of those around them

- That courage is seen in a pastor who prayerfully seeks God's priorities for ministry, and who is not deterred from acting upon those priorities by distracting demands.

- It is seen in the members of a church board that envision the ministry God has for their church and make that ministry the centerpiece of their monthly agenda, rather than dwelling on a disgruntled member or the latest problem with the building.

- This courage is seen in a church that does not allow its ministry to degenerate into responding only to the concerns of those within its walls, but seeks to permeate the surrounding community with the good news of Jesus Christ.

God looks into Joshua's heart for that courage. He also looks into your heart.

What if, in a moment of excitement, Joshua shares with the people God's vision for them, then a few days later begins to waver in his commitment? Commitment climbs when people see consistent passion in the person out front. Commitment is contagious. But if the rigorous demands that accompany the launching of a movement of God discourage this leader early on, he will lose credibility with the people. More importantly, the people will conclude that the vision God revealed was just "another good idea" that has no lasting impact. As a leader:

- you must be able to perceive the "new thing" God is doing;

- you must be able to see the territory He wants you to conquer;

- you must courageously act upon what God has shown you.

Others will be warmed as they get close to the fire that burns within your heart. Maximum influence begins with the level of your commitment.

Could you picture Dr. James Dobson with only a passing interest in matters related to the family? Can you imagine Charles Colson communicating that justice is "kind of" important and we ought to take a look at our prisons someday? How about Billy Graham only occasionally mentioning that the Bible has some good ideas in it and that people should possibly consider being born again? Think of Coach Bill McCartney suggesting that a man might want to make and keep some promises! Or John Maxwell suggesting ten ways to complete the sentence, "Everything rises and falls with—"!

No, God is using these men across our nation because of their commitment. Dr. Dobson courageously focuses on the family. Charles Colson makes us squirm as he prophetically highlights injustice and calls for change. Billy Graham passionately preaches that the Bible says, "You must be born again." Bill McCartney fills stadiums by challenging men to permit nothing to stand in the way of their promises. John Maxwell is raising up a generation of leaders with the contagious conviction that "Everything rises and falls with leadership." They invest their credibility every day to fulfill their God-given purposes.

Our circle of influence is certainly smaller than that of these national leaders, but the courage God requires is the same for all. Joshua had built up a certain amount of credibility with the Israelites. He had previously seen the land they were about to enter. He and Caleb had given a good report after spying out the land, and believed they could conquer it even when the majority doubted. He had been an aide to the spiritual giant Moses for as long as anyone could remember. Moses had publicly passed the torch to Joshua:

> "Now Joshua son of Nun was filled with the spirit of wisdom because Moses had laid his hands on him. So the Israelites listened to him and did what the Lord had commanded Moses" (Deuteronomy 34:9).

He was the chosen successor commissioned by Moses to lead the people where he could not. Now Joshua had to make a choice: Would he selfishly hoard his credibility and simply enjoy the perks of his place of leadership, or would he courageously invest his credibility to see that God's will was done?

Any credibility you have accumulated because of past accomplishments or faithfulness should be courageously offered to God. You must exercise the stewardship of credibility, just as you are to be a good steward of your time, talent and treasures. To hoard it, or to foolishly spend it, is to squander a God-given resource. You are to invest it so that others might be influenced to obey God.

There is a direct relationship between internal strength and external influence. That's obvious in churches. If a church is spiritually anemic or riddled with internal conflict, its ability to influence the community (or even its own youth!) is minuscule. If a church is spiritually vibrant and unified, its vision is contagious. The relationship between internal strength and external leadership is seen also in individual leaders. If personal insecurities cause leaders to selfishly pursue their own personal agendas, their circle of influence will diminish. If they courageously invest their own credibility in the future plans of God, their lives result in influence with eternal consequence.

I have come to believe that:

If you have courage, you will influence people based on your **convictions**.

If you lack courage, you will influence people based on your **comfort zones**.

Courage will take you anywhere you believe God is leading you. Without courage you will go only where you are comfortable. Will your leadership commitments be based on your convictions or on your comfort?

Our staff has developed some questions to use as indicators of whether we are choosing comfort over conviction:

1. Am I becoming protective of my ministry "turf"?

   One of the primary tasks of spiritual leaders is to raise up new leaders. If I am becoming indispensable or irreplaceable, it's a sign I'm more interested in my future security than in empowering others to be involved in ministry.

2. Am I no longer evaluating my ministry effectiveness?

   Personal evaluation of one's ministry along with the constructive criticism of others is necessary to refine any endeavor for God. When I start avoiding an honest critique of my programs or accountability for my actions, I'm choosing what's most comfortable.

3. Am I "emotionally exiting" my ministry?

   Sometimes difficulties wear us down and we decide to take a break by convincing ourselves that "we just won't care anymore." We go through the motions without the passion, because when problems arise it's more comfortable to be apathetic than emotionally invested in resolving them.

4. Am I unwilling to risk failure?

   It's most comfortable to only attempt what will be a sure success. However, most people and churches that are trying new things will experience some failures along the way. True change is not a risk-free proposition.

5. Am I opting for the familiar over the new?

   Am I trying new things, stretching my mind with new thoughts and building my skills by learning new approaches? Growth comes from seeking outside resources and being a continual, lifelong learner. Doing what has always been done is comfortable, yet erodes the impact of my ministry.

6. Am I only associating with people whose leadership skills are less developed?

One of the ways we grow is by learning from people who are where we need to be in the future — they are at the point where we would like to be someday. I'm choosing the comfortable when I only choose to be with people who learn from me.

7. Am I hanging on to, rather than giving away, ministry opportunities?

Each year I should seek to give away to others some of what I am currently doing and pick up some new responsibilities. Our staff has a goal to annually give away 20% of what we have been doing in the past and replace it with things we must start doing for the future. It's more comfortable to hang on to current responsibilities, because we've already developed those skills.

8. Am I fulfilling the role the church needs, or simply the role I like?

Leaders recognize there are various roles that must be filled in order for an organization to remain healthy and not develop blind spots. A leader must ensure that those roles are in place.

Let me illustrate. At one point our church board positions were filled by people who tended to be conservative financially. They regularly reviewed cash flow scenarios and budget projections, and any new ministry or building initiative was carefully tested against our financial capacity. I filled the role of "cheerleader" — trying to increase their comfort with risk and helping them to take bold steps. As time passed, the membership of our board changed. Most members were no longer fiscally conservative, and at times seemed even disinterested in financial matters. They were ready to "go for it," trusting that the finances would be there. My role had to change from cheerleader to "red flag raiser," pointing to the financial ramifications of decisions we were making. Which role would I rather play? Cheerleader. Which role needed to be played? That changed with the constituency of the board. A leader seeks to determine what role is needed, and either fills that role personally or encourages another to fill it. Courage chooses the role that is needed, not the one that is personally preferred.

9. Is false humility masking my insecurity?

It can appear like humility not to accept certain leadership positions or not to be involved in particular initiatives. We must always test our hearts to see if this is true humility, or simply a cover up for not doing something that is outside our comfort zone.

All of us occasionally answer these questions positively. We all retreat to our comfort zones when we feel threatened or overwhelmed. But when saying yes to these questions becomes the pattern of our leadership, it's time for a gut check.

Over the years our church has experienced some significant growth. By our sixteenth anniversary we'd begun our sixth building program. I've discovered that a growing church always requires more money. There's an ongoing need for additional staff and programs. I've come to recognize that I will be continually raising money for something!

Asking for money is one of those areas that has a high "cringe" factor. Like fingernails on a blackboard, the discussion of financial need is not music to most people's ears. The higher the "cringe" factor, the greater the investment of credibility by the leader. So one of the ways I must regularly re-invest whatever credibility I have accumulated is by financially challenging our congregation.

As a matter of conviction, I have no problem with issuing a financial challenge. I believe God wants His people to invest in His work. I believe that giving on earth results in treasures in heaven. I believe spiritual vitality is linked to generosity — that a person's heart is found in what he or she treasures. But as a matter of comfort, it's another story. The myth that "what a person gives is between him and God" is widely held in our community. I do not relish the opportunity of infringing on what another person considers to be a private matter.

So I must regularly make a choice. Will my leadership be based on my comfort zones, causing our church to be short of the necessary funds and our members deprived of a meaningful challenge to good stewardship? Or will my leadership be based upon conviction, transcending my comfort zones to do what is right and empowering people to be part of a movement of God? Comfort or conviction. I regularly face that choice. So do you. It's a matter of courage.

Courage For Obedience

Once again God challenges Joshua to "be strong and courageous" (1:7-8). This time, however, it is not the courage to influence others, but the courage to carefully obey God's Word. Meditating on it and doing everything in it are the pathways to true success and prosperity. A spiritual leader must be capable of receiving truth from God. Comprehending biblical truth and living it out increases spiritual authority, which is the basis of spiritual leadership.

Stephen Covey is the author of the widely read book, *The Seven Habits of Highly Effective People*. In it he speaks of the demands of leadership in a changing world. He is convinced that the ability to go through the change process or to make the necessary changes comes from having a "changeless core." That core is nurtured through values and principles that remain consistent even when the winds of change are blowing.[2]

For the Christian leader, those values and principles are revealed in God's Word. The Bible's lasting truths become embedded in our hearts through **meditation** — "meditate on it day and night" (1:8). There is no substitute for the reading and memorization of the Bible.

My personal accountability goals include a commitment to read through the Bible each year. I must admit that sometimes the daily readings don't seem to be even remotely relevant to my world. I've skipped a few sections of the genealogies and a few of God's pronouncements against nations that no longer exist. But I try to read most of it, and along the way am challenged by truths I otherwise might have missed. For instance, while writing these words I'm wading through the prophecies of Isaiah. As I've recorded my impressions in my journal, I've observed:

- It's dangerous to substitute dependence upon any human alliance for dependence upon God.

- Becoming proud and taking credit for victories that were brought about by the sovereign will of God is a sure way to encounter God's wrath.

Now alliances with Egypt or the punishment of Assyria may not be today's news, but the principles evident in them are worth meditating upon and incorporating into the changeless core of my life.

The Christian leader also integrates truth into his or her life through the **application** of God's Word — "be careful to *do* everything written in it" (1:8, emphasis added). The Bible determines how we act and react in the variety of life situations. A full life is lived from the inside out, and success comes as we obediently pursue God's best:

- If you want a better marriage, learn to love unselfishly and responsively (Ephesians 5:22-33).

- If you want a better relationship with your children, devote yourself to learning godly ways of instructing them without exasperating them (Ephesians 6:4).

- If you want more freedom or a promotion at work, serve wholeheartedly and work consistently no matter who is present or absent (Ephesians 6:5-8).

How you act toward your spouse is not based on how he or she acts toward you. Your treatment of your children is not determined by their treatment of you. Your day's work is not regulated by how the boss treats you or what other employees are doing. You must be careful to do what is written in God's Word. Consistent meditation and application bring about internal transformation. Living inside out means allowing God to change you, not excusing your behavior until God changes someone else!

"Be careful to obey . . . do not turn from it to the right or to the left. . ." (1:7). This is one of many commands in Scripture that call for focused obedience:

- "Do not turn aside from any of the commands I give you today, to the right or to the left, following other gods and serving them" (Deuteronomy 28:14).

- "He did what was right in the eyes of the Lord and walked in all the ways of his father David, not turning aside to the right or the left" (2 Kings 22:2).

- "Let us hold unswervingly to the hope we profess, for he who promised is faithful" (Hebrews 10:23).

What are the keys to that kind of obedience, that unswerving commitment to a life of integrity before God?

Like you, I am alarmed by the number of pastors who fail morally. Not only does this devastate their own relationship with God, but it has a disillusioning effect on the lives of so many others. Studies have shown that moral failure takes place when two things are true. The first is a neglect of quiet times in God's Word and prayer. The second is the lack of close relationships and accountability. It's hard to stay the course when flying solo. But consistent prayerful meditation on the Word of God and close relationships that provide accountability help reinforce unswerving obedience.

Like Joshua, God wants us to be courageously committed to wholehearted obedience. The internal victories of obedience to God will develop the character necessary for the external victories that are yet to come.

Courage For Perseverance

"Be strong and courageous. Do not be terrified; do not be discouraged. . ." (1:9). This is a call for courage that pursues the purposes of God over the long haul. This perseverance can be undermined by two powerful emotions — fear and discouragement.

What are some of the most common fears faced by spiritual leaders?

- Fear of failure. This one especially haunts those with perfectionist tendencies. In our church leadership team, we make it clear that we expect a failure once in a while. If everything we try must be a guaranteed success, the likelihood of a cutting edge ministry is remote.

  Over the years we've created quite a list of things we'll probably never try again. I've discovered, however, that while these attempts may not have turned out as we envisioned, they often ultimately led to some of the best ministries we have ever developed. It takes courage to try it, watch it fall, assess the reasons for its failure, have a good laugh about it, and learn what you need to know so you can try again.

- Fear of the unknown. "We've never done it that way before" can be a symptomatic reaction based on this fear. Just as the familiar is more comfortable, it is also less intimidating.

  When we first began our Saturday evening worship service, I remember the apprehension I felt about whether it would be a success. Our conservative community with a heavily Reformed influence was known for its commitment to Sunday as a day of worship. But our three worship services on Sunday morning were not accommodating all who wanted to worship with us, and did not allow us the necessary freedom to develop a significantly different approach to worship. So we ventured into the unknown, and God has blessed our Saturday evening service.

- Fear of a new level of commitment. Leadership in a movement of God committed to taking new territory will inevitably involve steps of personal growth. It's hard to make the necessary changes that allow us to be continually available for what God wants to do in the future.

  I've discovered that every time God wants to do something new through me He also does something new in me. The changes required within can be even more harrowing than the changes required in the surrounding circumstances.

It will take courage for Joshua to fight the battles that lie ahead. . . and the battles that lie within. God reassures Joshua that he need not be terrified. God will be with Him (and you) every step of the way.

"Do not be discouraged." Discouragement seems to come in two forms:

- Dis - courage: This is to be drained of courage. It's when circumstances of life or the criticism of people leaves you empty. It's variously referred to as burn-out or dryness of soul. You're unable to muster the internal fortitude necessary to take the next steps.

- Dys - courage: This is dysfunctional courage. It is when we create cheap substitutes for the real thing. It is when we inflate our ego or become insensitive in order to rise above the circumstances of life or the criticism of people. It is the beginning of pride that eventually invites confrontation from our God who "opposes the proud."

It is a blessing to witness a spiritual leader with a full heart, great courage and a small ego. Humility is not the opposite of courage; it is a prerequisite for it.

It will take great courage to persevere in the plan God has for you. It is a myth that, "If God is in it, things will happen easily, naturally and quickly." In reality, even people and churches who are pursuing God's will have problems that will require tremendous courage to endure. We cannot choose whether or not we'll have problems. We can only choose whether the problems we encounter will be those that accompany obedience, or those that accompany disobedience.

I'm convinced we need a theology of suffering to accompany our vision for leadership. Many people falsely assume, "If I'm doing God's will, I'll have health and wealth." The question courage asks is, "If I'm doing God's will, and experience pain and poverty, would I still do God's will?" That's the bridge Jesus crossed in the Garden of Gethsemane. That's the commitment Paul made as he sat in prison. That's the attitude John exhibited while exiled on the Island of Patmos. That's courage.

Ray and Anne Ortlund have written a little book entitled *You Don't Have To Quit.* In it they detail the lives of biblical characters who encounter three "zones."

The "A" Zone. This marks the initial days of service to God, and is characterized by the desire to achieve. It's the "honeymoon," when everything is new and expectations are high.

The "B" Zone. This time period is marked by the desire to quit. Initial expectations have proven idealistic. Reality begins to set in and problems begin to emerge. There is an almost irresistible urge to exit the situation or relationship.

The "C" Zone. This last period is experienced after moving through the "B" zone, and is characterized by the desire to grow and continue on. It is the most mature of the three zones.[3]

The applications are obvious. We see these "zones" in marriage relationships, in careers, and in church leadership. There are scores of people who love obeying God in the "A" zone but who quickly exit when the "B" zone is entered. It takes courage to persevere through the fear and discouragement present in the "B" zone and to finally come to the place of greatest effectiveness in service to God — the "C" zone.

I remember early in my ministry being puzzled by the frequency with which pastors left their churches immediately after a building program. I now understand that while those who watch from a distance may view a new building as simply exciting, those who provide leadership in making it happen may encounter conflicting expectations, financial pressures, long hours and tough decisions. "What looks exciting on the surface can be exhausting behind the scenes." It takes courage to persevere.

One of the greatest gifts we can give each other is encouragement. Like Barnabas in the New Testament, it would be an honor to have the reputation of being an encourager. That comes as we believe the best about others and generously express our support of them as they develop their relationship with God.

But the greatest encouragement can never come to us from another person. It arises out of our relationship with God. Others can't make up the deficit if we fail to experience the courage He wants to build into our lives through our quiet times with Him and His presence with us. I remember a seminar speaker who observed, "Most pastors have been taught to be caring, but they've never been taught to be courageous." I can think of no greater teacher than the Holy Spirit, "the Spirit of truth . . . [who] will guide you into all truth" (John 16:13). "Be strong and courageous."

Personal Reflection

1. This chapter mentions the passionate convictions held by men like Billy Graham and Bill McCartney. What is my passion? What people group or cause captures my heart with a compelling burden?

2. Joshua had to have the courage to transcend his personal comfort zones and invest his own credibility to move God's people forward. Can I think of a time when God asked me to invest my personal credibility to further His mission?

3. Success comes through meditation upon and application of God's Word (Joshua 1:8). How consistent are my times of Bible reading? Have I developed a goal for Scripture memory? Do I keep a journal in order to record what God may be saying to me through His Word?

4. Reflect on the A-B-C zones identified by the Ortlunds. In which zone would I currently place my walk with God? My marriage? My ministry?

Inventory for Spiritual Leaders

1. What are ways in which your church might increase its influence in the surrounding community? It may help to target specific areas, such as increasing influence with local government leaders, school personnel or the business community.

2. How would you describe the current heartfelt passion of your church? (Possibilities might include holiness, families, youth ministry, caring, teaching God's Word). Is this the passion you want to be the identifying mark of your church?

3. What decisions currently face your church that will require courage and perhaps the investment of the personal credibility of the leaders?

4. In which "zone" is your church currently: A, B or C?

5. Additional Reading: *Staying Power* by Ray and Anne Ortlund.[4]

Joshua's Journal

Lord, I'm grateful for the credibility you've entrusted to me. Since I have a limited supply, help me to invest it courageously but wisely. Grant me the courage to not only see Your vision, but commit to doing my part in making it a reality — even if it involves suffering. My desire is to consistently follow Your path without veering to the left or right. Please empower me to "stay the course." Amen.

FOOTNOTES

1. Raymond C. and Anne Ortlund, *Staying Power* (Nashville: Oliver and Nelson Books, 1986), p. 112.
2. Stephen R. Covey, *The Seven Habits of Highly Effective People* (New York: Simon & Schuster, 1989).
3. Raymond C. and Anne Ortlund, *You Don't Have to Quit* (Nashville: Oliver-Nelson Books, 1988.)
4. Ortlund, *Staying Power.*

Momentum is developed when we choose a team of people and obtain "Agenda Agreement" to move ahead.

Momentum is drained by going it alone or carelessly selecting the team members.

Chapter Four

Moving Forward Together

"Vision helps leaders get people very different from the leader and one another to pull together for a common purpose. Failure to build shared vision is the biggest mistake that gifted leaders can make."[1]

Bill Easum

Joshua's Journal 1:10-18

"In all my prayers for all of you, I always pray with joy because of your **partnership** in the gospel from the first day until now . . ." (Philippians 1:4-5, emphasis added).

When I was growing up, the neighborhood kids used to gather in a field behind our house to play baseball. It always started with the two best

57

players choosing sides. The process seemed to take forever, especially for those who were chosen last! One player would make his selection, then the other his selection. Back and forth it went until all were chosen and the teams were formed.

I was usually chosen toward the last, if not the very last. That bothered me. What annoyed me even more was that one of the kids was chosen before me even though I was the better player. There was a good reason for that — his parents owned a pool. The team he played on got to go swimming after the game! I learned that selections weren't always based on performance — sometimes there were some "politics" involved. He who has the pool makes the team.

Even though I know that "outside factors" sometimes affect who makes the team, I remain convinced that the greatest accomplishments for the kingdom of God will be team efforts. Dreams of divine origin are rarely achieved by "going it alone." While individual efforts in many sports may be admirable, God has placed us together in the body of Christ. We need each other. We cannot function without each other (1 Corinthians 12:12-27).

Joshua has come to understand that the old chapter of Israel's history is closing and God has chosen to do a new work through him. He's glimpsed the vision of the Promised Land that God is determined to give His people. He has been challenged by God Himself to "be strong and courageous." Now it's time to go public, to develop a team of people who will initiate God's plan for His people.

I can relate to Joshua. In 1979 , Dick Wynn and I saw the vision God laid on our hearts for a new church in the Kentwood community. After personally committing ourselves to this vision, we began to identify others who might launch this new church with us. One day we sat in his office, a legal pad on the desk and pens in hand, brainstorming the names of those we wanted to personally approach with this vision. There were no programs and no building. We had never met for worship. There were no guarantees. We would need people who believed in God, believed in our leadership and were willing to take a risk. We needed a team.

Joshua had an advantage. He had officers he could order to get the people moving (1:10). However, a closer look reveals he understood the crucial dimensions of team recruitment. He also understood how indispensable the issue of "promise" was to the team that would initiate this new movement of God.

A Team That Shares In God's Promises

God reveals His promises and His plans in different ways. For some, through meditation in God's Word and prayer, there is a sense of "hearing from God." Not an audible voice, but an internal conviction that they sense where God is leading and must obey. This is how Joshua received his direction from God, just as Moses had before him.

At other times God reveals His plans through another person. Perhaps this is how most people come to have an opportunity to become part of a movement of God. A leader like Joshua senses a direction from God and shares that direction with others. Those he shares with must determine if they believe the vision he senses is from God, and whether they are convinced they should be part of it. What is the process by which a leader shares his vision and people determine their response to it?

Waiting

Joshua orders the officers to go through the camp to tell the people that "three days from now" they will cross the Jordan River and enter the land God has promised. Why three days? Some have offered practical explanations. Maybe that's the time required for them to pack up. Perhaps it allows time for the spies Joshua sends out to complete their mission (2:22). Others have offered theological reasons, suggesting it may correspond to the three days Jesus spent in the tomb between His crucifixion and His resurrection. I believe there is another reason.

It is a waiting period. Their leader has told them what he believes God is leading them to do. Now it's time for the reality of what lies ahead to sink in. It's a time for them to decide whether they will "own" the vision and be part of it. It's a time to weigh the cost and test their willingness to pay the price to have God's very best — the Promised Land.

I remember when we first approached the people we would ask to become leaders in this new church. We organized our presentation to them and visited in their homes. We shared with enthusiasm how God had led us to this point. In my youthful zeal, I wanted to "close the sale" right on the spot — strike while the iron was hot! Dick Wynn made it clear we would lay out the vision and then leave, asking them to prayerfully consider their involvement. We would get back to them in a few days to hear their response. Dick was wisely seeking lasting commitments not based on an enthusiastic presentation but an internal conviction that could only grow in their hearts through prayer — the same way it had grown in our hearts.

Joshua announced confidently where God was leading. I'm sure there were people who wondered if he'd really heard from God or had eaten some day-old manna that caused him to have unusual dreams. Maybe there were some people who left camp, packing up and exiting so they wouldn't have to cross the Jordan River. The majority concluded that this was a mission from God and they wanted to be part of it. It was not just a promise to Joshua, but a promise to them. They came to share in God's promise "of the land the Lord **your** God is giving **you** for **your** very own" (1:11, emphasis added).

Recently our church went through a waiting period that tested the depth of commitment to the vision we believed God had given us. When we received the bids for the construction of our new sanctuary we were shocked. They came in 50% higher than the original estimates! The next Sunday we announced to the congregation the news we'd received. We could feel the reality set in. We invited our people to join us in prayer and "waiting upon the Lord." We were convinced we had designed the building that was right for our future ministry, and equally convinced we shouldn't borrow more money to meet the additional costs.

As we worked through this waiting period, we came to value the statement, "Where God has put a comma, we dare not put a period." Banners hung in our current worship center announcing, "It's a comma, not a period." God used that time to lead us to a new action plan and a very generous financial response from our congregation. More importantly, He used that time to develop our dependence upon Him.

Did everyone stay with us during this time and agree with the direction we sensed God was leading us? No. Some concluded they could not support the direction the congregation was going and chose to leave. It wasn't because they weren't spiritual — in fact, most of them were mature Christians who had hearts for God. It was because they had determined that our church's future direction was not where God was leading them personally, and chose to attend other churches. That was a bit painful for us. But, for most, God deepened their conviction that the direction we had chosen was His plan, and strengthened their commitment to make that vision become a reality. It took a waiting period to accomplish it.

When you share your vision with people, give them time to adjust. This isn't lost time. It may be the most valuable investment of time you ever make. Like waiting on a launch pad while the countdown is underway, it's preparation for expending the energy necessary to get a new initiative off the ground. Waiting is hard, but believing while waiting is harder still — and often necessary for God to do His work.

Communicating

Joshua also ordered his officers to communicate God's promises to the people. "Go through the camp and **tell** the people" (1:11, emphasis added) what they need to do in order to prepare to receive God's promised land. This process of communication is probably the most efficient way to spread the word about what is happening. It serves as well to broaden the leadership base beyond Joshua. Perhaps most importantly, every time the leaders (officers) communicate what God is going to do, they come to own it and understand it a little more.

We learn as we listen. But as any teacher knows, we also learn by passing to others what we have heard or read. Every time someone asks a question, a careful answer makes it clearer not only to the one asking the question but also to the one giving the answer. It is a wise leader who invites others to be part of the communication process. The Apostle Paul demonstrated this wisdom when he wrote to Timothy, "The things you have heard me say in the presence of many witnesses entrust to reliable men who will also be qualified to teach others" (2 Timothy 2:2). Notice the movement of communication:

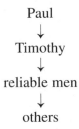

Paul
↓
Timothy
↓
reliable men
↓
others

It is the means by which God spreads His truth. It is also the means by which God spreads His vision.

At our church the board members take part in teaching the membership class. It not only benefits our new members, but is a healthy refresher for our board. When our telecare lay ministers make calls to our congregation and community, they are sometimes asked questions they are unable to answer. They seek out that answer and get back to the person, and two people have more fully learned about the church — the caller and the asker. In our "congregational chats" about ministry initiatives or building expansions, lay leaders as well as pastors make presentations and respond to the issues raised. Both leaders and attenders more clearly grasp what is coming next.

Joshua's leaders share in God's promises as they communicate them to others. Maybe that's why the Bible identifies one of the qualifications of a leader as "[the ability] to teach" (1 Timothy 3:2). Teaching is not the ability to stand in front of a class and lecture, but the ability to pass on to others God's Word and work.

Participating

Joshua orders the leaders to spread the word. The people are given the task of getting the supplies ready so they can move out. Everyone has a part. Everyone is participating in some way. Everyone is making a contribution to this new movement of God. People work through change, and Joshua is giving them something to work on. The successful completion of numerous small tasks will culminate in being poised to share in God's promise.

Joshua is an excellent delegator, and that's important for two reasons. First, it keeps him from spreading himself too thin and becoming too scattered. Second, it gives the people of God he is leading a sense of involvement in what God is doing. Good delegation lets people feel a little more in control of circumstances and events. It builds their sense of belonging and participation, and their commitment to carrying out the change.

Could you imagine Joshua trying to pack up the camp himself? He would work himself to the point of exhaustion while people stood around with nothing to do. The more time that passed with people standing idly by, the greater the likelihood that complaining would begin. Between Joshua trying to do it all and the people doing nothing but complaining, they'd spend another 40 years in the desert!

Maybe Joshua learned the importance of delegation from his mentor, Moses. Moses was a do-it-yourselfer until he was confronted one day by his father-in-law, Jethro. After watching Moses' attempts to handle every situation that arose among the Israelites, Jethro engaged Moses in this conversation:

> "'What is this you are doing for the people? Why do you alone sit as judge, while all these people stand around you from morning to evening?' Moses answered him, 'Because the people come to me to seek God's will. Whenever they have a dispute, it is brought to me, and I decide between the parties and inform them of God's decrees and laws.' Moses' father-in-law replied, 'What you are doing is not good. You and these people who come to you will only wear yourselves out'" (Exodus 18:14-18).

Moses was worn out, and the people were equally exhausted and frustrated because Moses could only be in one place at one time.

This is the way many churches operate. The pastor does it all while the people watch on the sidelines, only to complain when the pastor is not readily available. Or a few lay leaders are exhausted because they tackle every task, great or small. This sets an atmosphere that is conducive to burnout for the few and rustout for the rest.

Creating an environment of shared ownership of the vision and shared leadership in the task involves giving people the opportunity to contribute. Not everyone will be an "officer" who spreads the word. Some are gifted to be helpers in "getting the supplies ready." Getting a job done carries its own sense of reward. Achieving a task, especially a tough one, warms the heart and feeds the spirit. It also breeds commitment.

Years ago a formula that describes the change process was developed:

$$D \text{ (Dissatisfaction)} \times V \text{ (Vision)} \times F \text{ (First steps)} > R \text{ (Resistance)}$$

It says that dissatisfaction with the way things are, a vision for how they could be, and some first steps to make that vision a reality must be greater than the natural resistance people have to change. If any of those three (dissatisfaction, vision or first steps) are missing, people will resist the change.

Is this formula as old as Joshua?

Dissatisfaction: 40 years of desert wandering, the death of Moses.

Vision: "I will give you every place where you set your foot."

First Steps: "Get your supplies ready."

Joshua helps them to overcome the resistance to change and become part of a movement of God by giving them some practical, attainable steps to get them involved in what God is doing. We can learn from him. If we are dissatisfied with the way things are (it's time to close that chapter) and have a vision for how they should be (a clear statement of our preferred future), then we need to provide some ways in which everyone can be involved in the promises of God.

Joshua is careful not to build this movement around himself or the promises he can make. He leads people to share in the promises of God — ". . . go in and take possession of the land the **Lord your God is giving you** for your own" (1:11, emphasis added). To make it perfectly clear, he repeats it twice in nearly identical words (1:13, 15). He's building a team that shares in God's promises.

A Team Of People That Keeps Its Promises

Joshua next turns his attention to the two-and-a-half tribes that had made a special arrangement with Moses (1:12-16). These tribes wanted to settle east of the Jordan river because they felt the land was suitable for their very large herds and flocks (see Numbers 32). Moses felt this would divide the people of Israel and make it impossible for them to conquer the

Promised Land. They swore to him that they would leave their families and flocks behind, cross the Jordan River and help the rest of the tribes claim their inheritance in the Promised Land, and then return home. Moses agreed to this plan.

Now Joshua is reminding them of their promises. I admire them because they could have offered some excuses that are pretty common in today's society:

1. Too much time has passed — things have changed.

   In the time since they made their promise to Moses, their herds and families would have grown, so their responsibilities would have changed. Even Moses, the one to whom they had made the promise, was now dead.

2. They already had what they wanted.

   They have their "promised land" suitable for their purposes. They were not to receive one acre of the land they fought for on the other side of the Jordan River.

3. There would be too many sacrifices.

   They would miss time with their families. Their flocks and herds would be neglected. They would be risking their lives in battle.

Have you heard those excuses? Those who bow out of their marriage because "we were just kids, and so much has changed." Those who change their commitment once they have what they want. Or those who change their minds the first time they encounter sacrifice.

God builds His movement through people who keep their promises. I don't think it's a coincidence that one of the greatest spiritual movements of our day is called Promise Keepers. It is a movement which calls men to stand by the commitments they have made to God. If Joshua shares the vision with people, he wants to know they are people he can count on. He wants to fight the coming battles side-by-side with people who keep their word, not those who will exit at the first sign of difficulty.

One note of caution. We've all been disappointed by people who did not keep their word. It can be disillusioning to discover the person you thought was a spiritual giant is nothing more than a hypocrite. But don't let your disappointment with one person taint your perspective of all people. Godly movements are built on trust, and trust involves the risk that someone will disappoint you. Many have concluded that they will never trust again, and so hide their hearts (and their vision) behind walls they build to protect themselves.

Joshua has experienced his share of disappointments. After his participation in the spy mission commissioned by Moses, people he had trusted to give a good report gave a bad one (Numbers 13:32). He knows what it is like to have people reject his perspective (Numbers 14:6-10) and end up representing a minority position in a decision that will dramatically affect his future. Yet he continues to seek out people who **do** keep their promises.

It's worth noting that both Joshua and Moses realized it would take every fighting man of Israel to claim the land that God was about to give them. Their vision was big enough that nine-and-a-half tribes couldn't do what it would take. A God-given vision requires the whole team. Everyone in the body of Christ must function. I regularly tell our congregation we have a vision from God that cannot afford the luxury of "spectators." We need everyone's prayers, everyone's spiritual gifts, everyone's financial stewardship. I also tell them if there ever comes a day when our vision has shrunk to the point we don't need them, I'll apologize — and then I'll pray until God enlarges the vision to the point that we can't do it without them once again!

A Team Of People That Makes Strong Promises

The final two verses of Joshua 1 record a declaration of allegiance. The men of Israel promise to follow Joshua until the victory is completely won. If anyone fails to keep that promise, the penalty is death. Now that's a strong promise!

Imagine attending a wedding, expecting the bride and groom to exchange the traditional vows — "for better, for worse, for richer, for poorer, in sickness and in health, until death do us part." Instead, they promise to stay together "for better, for worse, for richer, for poorer, in sickness and in health — and if I don't, you can kill me." The marriage rate would drop and the murder rate would climb!

Imagine signing a contract for a loan. The penalty for falling behind in payments is not the usual additional interest, but the threat of death. No escape through declaring bankruptcy in this contract! Loans would be fewer, and the default rate would decrease dramatically.

I'm not suggesting that the Israelites' pledge of "obedience unto death" should provide a pattern for all promises. It does, however, strongly express their commitment to doing whatever it takes to lay hold of the future vision God has given them. It also gives evidence of their willingness to submit to Joshua's authority and follow his leadership.

J. Robert Clinton, in his book *The Making of a Leader*, asserts that, "Leaders who have trouble submitting to authority will usually have trouble exercising spiritual authority."[2] Many people are attracted to leadership because of the power and prestige they believe it will provide. This attraction is often based in a proud spirit, which the Bible consistently declares invites the opposition of God. "God opposes the proud, but gives grace to the humble" (James 4:6). Spiritual authority is not humanly generated by a grasp for power but is obtained through a willingness to be a servant of all — beginning with submission to God. Spiritual authority is built on a foundation of humility, and a willingness to follow when God's plan calls for strong followers.

Their pledge of allegiance includes more than a commitment to follow. It contains words of encouragement. The words "be strong and courageous" were first given to Joshua by his mentor Moses (Deuteronomy 31:6, 7, 23). Then they were communicated directly from God to Joshua (Joshua 1:6, 7, 9). Now they are coming from those Joshua will lead. Joshua should certainly be getting the message by now!

When Recruiting A Team, Expect A Variety Of Responses

Sometimes leaders are surprised by the wide variety of reactions people have to their vision. Some naively assume that if a vision is from God, all the people who hear its presentation will respond positively. As I've shared our vision for ministry over the years, I've noticed five different types of responses:

1. Refreshers: These are people who inspire you to dream great dreams and attempt great things for God. They may encourage you through personal affirmation. Their investments in your life may enable you to reach higher than you would otherwise. I've noticed that some of the "refreshers" in my life don't even know me personally. By reading their books, hearing them speak or watching them in action, I'm inspired.

2. Refiners: They sharpen your ideas and clarify your vision. This might be accomplished through constructive criticism or through their ability to ask provocative questions. It happens through people who eagerly want to receive your vision, but can't quite seem to grasp it. As you struggle to make it clear to them, it becomes clearer to you.

3. Reflectors: Some people simply reflect your vision and energy. They don't create any energy themselves, nor do they detract from the momentum of your vision. They are usually agreeable, pleasant people to have around — they are faithful people.

4. Reducers: These folks seek to reduce your vision to their comfort

zones. They resist the areas of your vision that represent what they consider to be undesirable changes. They may agree with the risk-free dimensions of your plan, but resist those which make them uncomfortable.

5. Rejecters: They will never adopt your vision. They will either exit, or stay and drag their feet in an attempt to frustrate you until you exit. They drain momentum and enthusiasm.

As I've encountered these various responses, I've drawn the following conclusions that help me in relating to them:

- I used to assume that I really needed the first two groups, I would enjoy the middle group, and I should watch out for the last two groups. I now believe that all responses are helpful in clarifying and communicating a vision.

- I've noticed that the first two groups are usually busy and productive people. If you want their input, you usually have to seek them out rather than wait for them to come to you. If you only respond to those who come to you, the feedback you receive may be skewed. Often it's those who feel most negative that are strongly motivated to make their feelings known. This is why many pastors spend almost all their time with negative people, and many church boards have agendas that are nothing more than responding to problems. I deliberately initiate appointments with people I believe will refresh and refine our church's vision.

- When you're drained of energy, it's easiest to spend your time with the "reflectors." These are nice people who are faithful, supportive and pleasant to be around. It's obvious that there might be a tendency to avoid the last two groups — the reduction or rejection of your vision causes a drain of energy. But there is also a tendency to avoid the people who stretch you or ask the probing questions — which if continued over a period of time is a prescription for mediocrity.

- Remember that the initial response to any substantive change is resistance. Another benefit of sharing your vision and allowing time for people to process it (the "waiting period" mentioned earlier) is that it permits them to work through the natural resistance that first arises. Don't label people as "rejecters" or "reducers" when they may, after working through a brief period of resistance, be your strongest supporters.

Expect a variety of responses. Just because you believe you have received a vision from God, don't assume people will receive it from you without a variety of responses. It takes wisdom to capitalize on each of these responses in order to make your vision a reality.

Recruiting a team is hard work, and yet it is some of the most necessary work for the leader. The potential within a church is directly related to its leadership team. In growing as a leader, be sure your team grows with you. If you're expanding as a church, monitor whether or not a corresponding expansion is taking place in the leadership base. Constantly equipping, enlarging and upgrading a team of leaders is an indispensable dimension of a movement of God.

Personal Reflection

1. Have I ever spent time in God's "waiting room"? If so, what did I learn during those experiences? Am I continuing to "wait upon the Lord" to give me direction or maturity and ministry?

2. The process for change was summarized as D x V x F > R, or Dissatisfaction x Vision x First steps must be greater than Resistance. Can I think of a time in my life when I was dissatisfied, and God used it to prompt positive change?

3. Have I made any promises on which I've not followed through? Do I need to renew that commitment or seek forgiveness for making an improper commitment?

4. Are there those who have hurt me by failing to keep their word? Have I allowed their failure to fester into bitterness in my heart, or have I sought to grant forgiveness?

5. Who are the people who "refresh and refine" my spiritual walk? Some I may know well (friends, fellow church members, etc.). Some I may not even know personally (authors, radio or television ministers, etc.).

Inventory for Spiritual Leaders

1. When forming ministry teams, what efforts do you make to discover the spiritual gifts, abilities and experiences of those being recruited? Does your recruitment simply fill vacancies, or is orientation given to those assuming places of service?

2. When launching a new ministry initiative, do you allow for a "waiting period" so God can impress the idea upon the hearts of others? Does your system of communication allow for feedback? Do you give several opportunities for people to participate in

different ways?

3. Do you trust your leadership teams to make decisions and carry out their responsibilities, or must they constantly check back with the pastor or church board to receive permission for almost everything they do?

4. Five different responses have been identified — refreshers, refiners, reflectors, reducers and rejecters. Do you know the people in your church who might belong to each group? Are you relating to the various types of responses in a way that best moves your church's vision forward?

5. Additional Reading: *Sacred Cows Make Gourmet Burgers* by William Easum.[3]

Joshua's Journal:

Lord, while the vision You've entrusted to me is personal, it is not private. Help me share it with others in such a way that Your Spirit is freed to build ownership for it in their hearts. I want to trust You, to wait upon You to convince people to be part of what You are doing. I submit to Your authority, and commit to using whatever spiritual authority You've delegated to me in a way that honors You. Keep me open to the variety of responses people will share, but please bring people to me who will move Your vision toward reality. Amen.

FOOTNOTES

1. *NEXT*, a publication of Leadership Network, Vol. 1, Number 3, October 1995, p. 2.
2. J. Robert Clinton, *The Making of a Leader* (Colorado Springs: NavPress, 1988), p. 101.
3. William Easum, *Sacred Cows Make Gourmet Burgers* (Nashville: Abingdon Press, 1995).

Momentum is developed through setting realistic goals and action plans.
Momentum is drained by failing to survey the obstacles and opportunities,
leaving blind spots in our plans.

Chapter Five

Time for a Reality Check

"Realistic leaders are objective enough to minimize
illusions. They understand that self-deception
can cost them their vision."[1]

Bill Easum

Joshua's Journal 2

"Now listen, you who say, 'Today or tomorrow we will go to this or that
city, spend a year there, carry on business and make money.' . . .Instead,
you ought to say, 'If it is the Lord's will, we will live and do this or that'"
(James 4:13, 15).

"**R**ejoice with those who rejoice; mourn with those who mourn"
(Romans 12:15). Serving as a pastor provides plenty of

opportunities for both. On more than one occasion I've left a joyful wedding celebration to officiate at a funeral. In one appointment I listen to a person share the joy of a dream come true. In the next I empathize with a person whose dream is irreparably broken. Ministry is a mixed bag of experiences.

From time to time people share with me their dreams of starting a new business. They talk about the freedom it will give them to be their own boss, the money they will make and the influence they will have on others. These stories intrigue me because of my own early desires to enter the business world. I delight in their dreams, but also sense another responsibility — to match them with others who have walked that road.

There are some harsh realities that commonly accompany the initiation of a new business. Those who envision being their own boss soon discover they will have many bosses, called "customers." Their business plans map a road to profitability in one year, when in reality it may require a decade to turn the first real profit. Others who have "been there and done that" can provide a reality check for them. These glimpses of reality should not limit or determine the vision, but can enlighten the potential business owner as to what it will take to accomplish the vision.

Likewise, spiritual leaders must make a realistic assessment of the obstacles and opportunities involved in a new step of faith. Sometimes this can be done by the leaders alone, but most times it is beneficial to garner the input of others. This "reality check" allows for the creation of relevant action plans to carry out a God-given vision.

Chapter two of Joshua records a spy mission organized by Joshua as the Israelites prepare to enter the Promised Land. He forms a "task force" of two and gives a clear mandate of what they are to accomplish. From Joshua and his spies we can learn the bases that need to be covered as we scout out new territory to be taken for God.

Check What You've Learned From Past Experience

This is not the first time spies were sent to scout the Promised Land. The last spy mission was initiated by Moses, and Joshua had been one of those spies (see Numbers 13 and 14). I believe Joshua 2:1 reflects some changes Joshua made as a result of past experience:

1. **Joshua sends the spies out *secretly*.**

    When Moses had sent out the spies, they were selected publicly and were allowed to give a public report (Numbers 13:26-33). This resulted in a disaster that cost a movement of God forty years of potential progress, perhaps for the following reasons:

- They reported to people who didn't have the faith or the vision to process the realities without being unduly frightened by them (Numbers 14:1-4).

- In that public setting the spies veered from their original mandate. Their commission was to provide *information* about the Promised Land (Numbers 13:17-20, 27-29), not their *opinion* about whether it could be done (13:31-33).

- Their official, public report (Numbers 13:26) degenerated into a subversive, negative report (13:32). The rebellious ten spies, capitalizing on their visibility and experience, spread among the Israelites a "bad" report.

Joshua sends the spies out secretly. They are not commissioned publicly nor are they ever given the opportunity to report publicly. They form a task force that is to provide him with information about the obstacles and opportunities of the Promised Land. He wants to see how much things had changed in the forty years since he had scouted the territory himself.

Observations for Today's Leaders: When forming a task force to investigate a new step of faith, determine if their report is to only include information, or are they to give an evaluation of the feasibility of this new step? It should be made clear how and to whom they are to report. Is their work to be somewhat confidential until those who have decision-making authority have had an opportunity to review and respond to their conclusions? It can be very beneficial when recruiting task force members to have a healthy up-front conversation about the report being given to the appropriate people. Underscore the negative impact of spreading the report to people who may not be ready to face the challenges until the leaders can give direction.

2. **Joshua sends out *two spies*.**

Moses had sent out twelve spies, one to represent each of the twelve tribes (Numbers 13:2-16). Their participation in the spy mission was based on their position in the tribal structure of the nation of Israel. It seemed to be a good idea to have a delegation representative of the people of God. Later, however, it becomes evident that only two of them (Joshua and Caleb) had the faith required to participate in such a mission. This resulted in changing God's guarantee of victory (13:2) into a "maybe."

Joshua sends out two spies. He is making the transition from leadership based on **position** (representatives from each tribe) to leadership based on **conviction** (a firm belief in God's promises). A glimpse of their faith is found in their later conversation with Rahab, where they promise to treat her kindly (if she upholds her end of the bargain) when the Lord gives them the land (Joshua 2:14). Not *if* the Lord gives them the land, but *when* He gives it.

Observation for Today's Leaders: Many times boards and committees are formed based on representation of various groups within the church. While this is great if there are enough people of faith to represent the various groups, this commitment can be disastrous if negative people are chosen just because of their position in a certain group. Many church boards, in an effort to have broader representation, have expanded in a way that results in diluted faith and needless wandering.

3. **Joshua focuses their efforts on *Jericho*.**

When Moses sent out the twelve spies, he gave them a broad assignment: to "explore the land" (Numbers 13:16-20). The assignment may have been too broad, resulting in a mission that took forty days to accomplish. They were gone so long they began to magnify the barriers and minimize the blessings (13:27-29). They began to weigh only the cost of doing something — of moving forward with God's plan. They lost sight of the cost of doing nothing — of standing still in disobedience to God's plan.

Police departments often use undercover officers to get the information they need. At times these officers can be out of contact with the department for an extended period of time. If this "deep" cover operation goes on too long, these officers may forget to whose authority they are accountable and in which world they really belong. The result may be the loss of officers and a failed mission.

Joshua commissions his task force to "look over the land," but "especially Jericho." The focus on Jericho allows them to complete their work in just a few days and return to their own people.

Observations for Today's Leaders: When creating a task force to provide realistic action plans that overcome the obstacles, carefully focus on their responsibilities and establish a realistic time frame. Nearly anyone who spends too much time focusing on financial, facility or personnel limitations can begin to lose faith. These limitations must be realistically identified yet not allowed to loom too large as a result of continual focus upon them.

Joshua learned from his past experiences. He did not ignore reality by skipping a spy mission completely. Like Jesus, he realized the wisdom of counting the cost (Luke 14:25-35). However, the way he structured the mission reflects the wisdom of experience. Spiritual leaders, when taking a new step of faith, should ask, "Have we tried anything similar in the past and what did we learn?" That willingness to learn from previous experiences develops wisdom and can prevent catastrophe.

Check Out What Others Have To Say

The spies embark on their mission and end up at the house of Rahab (2:1-7). Before the spies go to sleep for the night, Rahab goes up on the roof to talk to them. From their conversation with Rahab (2:8-11), the spies learn some things that must greatly encourage their hearts:

- She knows God has given them this land and that those who live there are melting in fear because of the impending invasion of God's people.

- The people of the land have heard what God has done to others who have tried to stand in the way of His plan (the Egyptians and the Amorites). They are well aware that the God of Israel has a track record of victory.

- Their hearts have melted and courage has failed, for "the Lord your God is God in heaven above and on the earth below" (2:11). The power of the God of Israel knows no boundaries.

Sometimes the confirmation of a movement of God comes from the most unexpected sources. This pagan woman and her people are probably more convinced of the power of God than the average Israelite is at this point!

A reality check involves listening to the viewpoints of others and actively seeking their input. There are different levels of listening. At the most superficial level, listening is focused on words alone. On a deeper level, listening moves beyond what is communicated verbally and an attempt is made to grasp what a person is feeling. This involves not only what is said, but the reason why it is said. But for the spiritual leader, there is yet a deeper level of listening. Beyond the words and feelings, it is looking for evidence that God is preparing the way for what He wants to do.

When Moses sent spies into the Promised Land forty years earlier, did they listen to the people of the land? Or did they so concentrate on the physical blessings and barriers that they missed the spiritual and invisible preparation that God had already accomplished?

To whom should we listen when conducting a reality check? When preparing for a major new initiative, I attempt to gather input from the following groups of people:

1. **Listen to people whose needs will potentially be met if the action is taken**. This helps me to determine if there is a "niche" for that ministry and what exactly needs to be accomplished to meet the need. It can be dangerous to assume that we know what people need, or to simply duplicate what has been done elsewhere to meet similar needs.

   For instance, when we began a new singles' ministry recently, we assumed that their desire would be to study issues and challenges particularly relevant to being a single adult. We soon discovered that our assumption was wrong. While the core group of this new initiative indicated it would be nice to have occasional seminars addressing needs particular to the single person, they wanted their ongoing class curriculum to focus on spiritual and emotional maturity for the Christian adult. These principles of spiritual formation are similar whether an adult is single or married. Listening to our singles helped us to correct our false assumptions before the ministry started off on the wrong foot.

2. **Listen to people who have the resources to meet the need**. These resources may be financial or spiritual gifts that address the need, or experience in ministry in that area. Just because a need exists, it does not mean that God is calling a church to meet that need. It's wise to evaluate available resources of people, space and finances.

   Many people over the years have offered suggestions regarding programs they would like us to offer. Often they are sharing with us something they have witnessed in another church or parachurch organization. We ask if they are willing to help initiate that ministry, and we may also voice the idea to others who might have the resources to help launch or sustain it. We've learned that if no one steps forward to provide leadership or support, it's best to place the suggestion in a "future idea" file until God raises up the required workers.

3. **Listen to people outside the walls of the church**. I regularly ask our community leaders what they perceive as needs in our city. I talk to unchurched people about what they see a church doing in that given area to meet the need. Sometimes I talk to other church

leaders in the community to see what they have tried to do or are currently doing.

At least once a year I seek an appointment with our city's mayor and Superintendent of Schools. They witness changes in our geographical area that help determine our approach to outreach. This keeps us from becoming ingrown by only listening to "insider information" found within our church leadership team.

4. **Listen to the skeptics**. These are the people who believe something can't or shouldn't be done. They'll point out the pitfalls and prejudices associated with a "new territory" of ministry. You don't have to agree with them, nor do you need to convince them they are wrong. You are simply learning what makes people uncomfortable and where resistance may be encountered.

For years we've conducted multiple worship services on Sunday morning. This is a trend that is picking up momentum as facility costs increase and people's desires for options also increase. When we adjust service times, we try to listen to people who don't like our suggested schedule. We try to discover why they are skeptical of it. This helps us anticipate problems and, when possible, nip them in the bud.

5. **Listen to people who have already done what you are considering**. Learn from their experiences as well as from your own. I've discovered that gleaning insights from the experiences of others can lead to having much better experiences yourself!

As we began the construction of our new sanctuary, I became concerned about the potential impact of moving into a sanctuary three times the size of our existing one. I conducted interviews with the leaders of others churches who had made similar transitions. I videotaped their responses to my questions about how the physical move had affected the "culture" of their churches. Among my discoveries:

- Their congregations struggled with the new building not "feeling" the same. The congregational singing wasn't as resounding because the new facility was roomier. The fellowship didn't seem as close because members were no longer bumping into one another in crowded hallways or packing the pews as tightly. Some people concluded that because the worship and fellowship didn't seem the same, God wasn't as "present" in the new facilities as He had been in the old.

- The expectations for every dimension of ministry were higher. The choir should sing better and the pastor should have better sermons in this "new and improved" sanctuary. This increase in expectations was subtle yet powerful, and led some to be disappointed with the ministry of the church. Like putting a familiar picture in a brand new frame, the ministry didn't look the same anymore.

- Some of the churches experienced a decrease in volunteerism. Lay ministers were intimidated and struggled with whether or not they were "good enough" to serve in the new surroundings. As the facilities influenced expectations, the volunteers' sense of inadequacy was amplified.

These are just a few of the insights I gleaned from their experiences. I have shown the videotape of these interviews to our board and our staff, hoping to anticipate the transitions our congregation will face and, thus, plan accordingly. It is true — we shape the design of our facilities, and then they shape us.

Choosing a cross section of people who view an initiative from different perspectives can provide a picture of whether God is preparing the way for that endeavor.

The need to be seeker-sensitive is widely discussed by churches today. Willow Creek Community Church and Pastor Bill Hybels have led the way, highlighting the needs of "unchurched Harry" to develop a focus for ministry. But Joshua's spies long ago demonstrated seeker-sensitivity by listening to the perspectives of "unchurched Rahab." They listened to her fears and her hopes. They listened to her view of their God and what they might do to meet her needs. Undoubtedly what they learned shaped their final report to Joshua.

Check To Be Certain All The Bases Have Been Covered

A reality check that only investigates one aspect of the anticipated initiative isn't a reality check at all. This "task force" of two spies seeks a vision of what is ahead that will cover all the realities. Their vision of the Promised Land is three-dimensional:

- A Vision of Condemnation (2:9-11)

They are given a glimpse of a world condemned by God. They witness the fear and despair of people who face judgment. With Rahab's help, they look beyond the defenses and defiance to see the lordship of God both in heaven and on earth, even in this pagan land. That is the beginning point of their vision, and should be the beginning point of any vision a church develops.

This vision of condemnation is very different from the common vision of society today. We live in a country that believes people are basically good. This, in spite of the Bible's clear teaching on the depravity of mankind and the abundant evidence in the daily news that man is capable of incredible evil. If the church's vision was in contrast to this view of the "goodness" of man, that would provide some hope. But even the church acts increasingly as if salvation is universal, and everyone will make it somehow. While this may not be publicly stated, many Christians fail to share their faith in their circles of influence, comforting themselves with the thought that their contacts will make it to heaven because they are basically "good" people.

Do we really believe that people who do not submit their lives to God end up in hell? Do we have a vision of people condemned if they don't take advantage of the opportunity to respond to God in repentance? At Kentwood Community Church, our leaders occasionally take tours of the surrounding community to allow God to break our hearts for people condemned apart from Christ. We drive to the schools and picture the eternal destiny of young people. We drive through wealthy neighborhoods and remind ourselves that money cannot provide salvation. We tour neighborhoods where poverty is present and remember that the greatest poverty is not financial, but spiritual. Every decision we make must include the reality of condemned people.

At times the book of Joshua is criticized because of the killing of the people who previously inhabited the land. What chances, however, would these people have had for eternal life if the Israelites had never invaded the land? Rahab makes it clear they already knew about God and could have chosen to submit to His plans. Every victory in the Promised Land is an opportunity for repentance — an opportunity for condemned people like Rahab to become consecrated people devoted to God and His purposes in the world.

• A Vision of Salvation (2:12-14)

Lost people matter to God. We must ask the question, "Were the spies only sent to check out the Promised Land in preparation for invasion?" While I'm convinced that was the primary purpose, I'm also convinced God spotted Rahab's faith from a long way off. This mission demonstrates the lengths to which God will go for the salvation of a soul and her family. God goes a long way for a little faith!

Spiritual leaders must remind themselves how much lost people matter to God. From the first verse most people learn (John 3:16) to the three parables Jesus shares in Luke 15 (the lost sheep, lost coin and lost son), the Bible emphasizes that God is in the business of seeking and finding lost people. The scarlet cord Rahab hangs from her window has been a symbol throughout church history of the blood of Christ shed for lost people. The reality of God's heart for the lost compels us to act courageously to reach them.

• A Vision of Action (2:17-21)

The spies commit themselves to the rescue of Rahab and her relatives. Their vision results in an action plan. Rahab acts on her faith by covering for the spies, hanging out the scarlet cord and gathering her relatives into her house. Her example of faith combined with works leads the New Testament writer James to include her as an example of faith in action (James 2:25).

While we must sense the brokenness of people in our world and the heart God has for them, the lack of realistic action plans never allows those feelings to mature beyond mere sentimentalism. The focus must move beyond how we feel about it to what we will do about it. A sense of conviction must culminate in a plan of action.

This three-dimensional vision is indispensable to any new ministry initiative. Without a vision for condemnation, we will not see the eternal difference our actions can make. Without a vision for salvation, we may judge the lost but not reach them. Without a vision for action, our faith is impotent. Like a three-legged stool, all legs must be present to support the taking of new territory.

Check Out All The Conditions Before Making Your Commitments

Rahab asked the spies for a commitment (2:12-13) to show kindness to her and her family by preserving their lives. The spies indicated their willingness to meet her request, but set certain conditions for their commitment:

• Rahab could not tell anyone what the spies were doing (2:14). She had to keep their mission a secret to prevent the residents of the land from making special preparations for their attack.

- Rahab had to hang a scarlet cord from her window (2:18). The spies might not remember the exact location of her house when they returned and could not be responsible for going house to house to find her when a battle was raging.
- Rahab had to gather into her house the family members she wanted saved from destruction by the Israelites (2:18). Not only would this be a demonstration of some level of faith among the family members, but it would be impossible to attempt to locate all of her relatives during the course of the battle.

While the spies were very grateful for what Rahab had done and greatly encouraged by her report of the preparatory work God had done, their enthusiasm did not result in unrealistic commitments. Their conditions answer questions that wise spiritual leaders ask, such as:

- What happens if another person does not do what he or she promised?

If Rahab did not uphold her end of the bargain, the deal was off. As church leaders, we need to ask, "What happens if people do not follow through on the financial pledges they have made? What happens if volunteers for a ministry back out? What happens if the space is no longer available?"

- Are my commitments realistic under the conditions?

The spies knew their promises would have to be kept in the midst of a battle. Spiritual leaders assess such conditions as available finances, time and willing volunteers as they make their commitments.

- Do my commitments obligate others, and am I authorized to speak for them?

The spies were obligating Joshua by their promise, and obviously had been given the right to speak for him. When a leader makes a commitment for others, he or she must be certain to have the authority to speak for those people.

These are the questions we asked when we were raising money and securing financial arrangements for our new sanctuary. We asked questions like these when we established a partnership with our denomination for planting new Wesleyan churches in Cambodia. Making realistic commitments requires an assessment of the conditions under which those commitments will be carried out.

Check To See If Your Conclusions Represent Both Facts and Faith

The spies return to Joshua and give their "task force" report (2:23-24). Their conclusions are an appropriate blend of fact and faith:

- Fact: They "told him everything that had happened to them."
- Faith: "The Lord has surely given the whole land into our hands; all the people are melting in fear because of us."

When pursuing God's purpose, both facts and faith are ne essary. What a challenge it is to determine the appropriate blend!

When we make decisions at our church, we seek to make **wise** decisions. Wisdom cannot be developed unless we relate God's perspectives to the realities of life. There is no such thing as blind faith. In fact, what makes Christian faith so unique is its ability to face the realities and yet have hope that transcends those realities. The most powerful example is the ability of Christians to face the awful intrusion of death upon God's design for life, and yet through God's grace realize that death is but sleep before they awaken in God's presence. In the same way, we can realistically face the obstacles of any new initiative and yet not be limited by them. The process of seeing God at work as we face the challenges develops wisdom.

We also seek to make **faith-stretching** decisions. We want to "take new territory for God" and move beyond our comfort zones. This faith is not ignoring the "reality check," but allowing God to lead us as we make our way through it.

Personal Reflection

1. As I review my personal journey with God, have I had the faith to see the obstacles and yet not be limited by them? What were some of those obstacles? How, by God's grace, were they overcome?

2. What have I learned from past experiences that is important to keep in mind for the future? If a new Christian were to ask me to share five lessons from my experience with the Lord, what would I share?

3. The conclusion of the spies Joshua sent included both the facts and faith (Joshua 2:23-24). Which do I more naturally lean toward — facts or faith? How do I compensate for this natural tendency in order to keep the fact/faith balance?

4. Are there areas in my life right now where God is asking me to "count the cost" (Luke 14:25-35)?

Inventory for Spiritual Leaders

1. Is there an area in your church's ministry where a task force would be helpful right now?

   If so: Who will they report to when they are finished, and how will that report be given?

   Is their assignment sufficiently focused?

   Have you been careful to select participants based on quality rather than quantity?

2. Is there an opportunity through a short-term assignment to "check out" future leaders?

3. If your church is about to take a step of faith (building program, multiple services, new program, etc.):

   Have you checked with others who have taken a similar step?

   Have you estimated the consequences of both taking the step and not taking the step?

   Have you listened to the various groups of people who may be impacted by it?

Joshua's Journal:

Lord, help me to learn from my experiences and yet not be limited by them. May I be objective enough to bring to the surface any self-deception that may cost me my vision. Guide me in discerning my weaknesses and grant me the security to surround myself with people and strengths to offset them. Amen.

FOOTNOTE

1. *NEXT*, p. 2.

Momentum is developed by humbly creating a movement focused on God and His authority.

Momentum is drained by pridefully establishing a man-centered movement.

Chapter Six

Focusing On Priorities

"It is extremely easy for us to give our major attention to minor things."[1]

E.C. McKenzie

Joshua's Journal 3

"Since, then, you have been raised with Christ, set your hearts on things above, where Christ is seated at the right hand of God. Set your minds on things above, not on earthly things" (Colossians 3:1-2).

During our Saturday night service, called "Night Life" (based on John 10:10), Rob shared his life story. He had grown up going to church. He had gone through the motions of making a commitment to Christ at various points in his childhood and teenage years. As his teen years progressed, he decided to stop pretending and to start "enjoying" life. He spent more and more time partying, his greatest point of pride being the amount of alcohol he could consume. He graduated from alcohol to marijuana, convincing himself that his daily use of it didn't mean he was a "pothead." It simply helped his aching body after a day's work on the cement crew.

During this time he met the girl he wanted to marry, and on a special occasion she wanted to give him a gift. He requested a gold cross to wear around his neck. It wasn't the religious nature of the symbol that made him choose a cross. He just viewed it as a cool piece of jewelry to wear on a daily basis. Little did he know the impact it would have on his life.

When he got ready for work in the morning, the cross was reflected in the mirror. When he prepared for bed at night, he felt the cross around his neck. It seemed to enlarge as time went on. He couldn't help but focus on it, and it became a powerful reminder of all he had learned in his childhood at church. He also became keenly aware of how out of sync his life was with what the cross represented. His growing attention to that cross was used by God to bring conviction to his heart, and finally commitment of his life to Christ.

What you focus on can influence the direction of your life. Focus can determine the difference between success and failure. I learned that while I was young. My dad would say, "Keep your eye on the ball," as he pitched baseballs to me. My grandpa would say, "Focus on that mark on the lane," as I threw my bowling ball down the alley. The teacher would say, "Keep your eyes on your own paper," as my classmates and I took a test.

Focus is important beyond the world of sports and school. Businesses that lose their strategic focus may see their profit margins disappear. Couples who fail to pay attention to their marriage slowly but surely become strangers. Organizations that lose sight of their mission statements soon wallow in mediocrity. Churches that fail to center on Christ trade a ministry of eternal consequence for activity with temporary impact.

Focusing on God can create great expectations that can lead to great endeavors. As Joshua prepares to move the people into the Promised Land, there is no mystery as to what the focal point is. It is the "ark of the covenant." Mentioned often in Scripture, this piece of Tabernacle furniture was approximately 5 feet long by 3 feet wide by 3 feet deep. In Joshua 3, the ark of the covenant is mentioned nine times in just seventeen verses. It symbolizes two important dimensions that are indispensable to all who seek to be part of a movement of God.

A Reference Point For God's People

As Joshua and the Israelites stand on the brink of the Jordan River, anticipating entry into the Promised Land, the officers go throughout the camp giving orders to the people: "When you see the ark of the covenant of the Lord your God, and the priests, who are Levites, carrying it, you are to move out from your positions and follow it. Then you will know which way to go, since you have never been this way before. . ." (3:3-4). The ark serves as a reference point, indicating when they are to move out and which way they are to go.

Notice where the focus is **not** directed. The officers do not focus attention on the obstacles. The Jordan River, which flows between the Israelite camp and the Promised Land, is not a meandering creek. It is at flood stage (3:15), likely flowing rapidly and making any crossing precarious. It would be easy for the people to be discouraged if their focus was on the obstacle just ahead. As mentioned in the last chapter, a "reality check" is important and obstacles need to be noted. But they are not the center of attention in any endeavor of faith.

It is also clear that the focus is **not** on Joshua, the officers or the priests. It is not centered on one leader or a small group of leaders. Any man-centered movement will achieve temporary success at best. Spiritual leaders demonstrate great wisdom when they fulfill their roles in a movement of God without seeking to become the center of attention. The temptation to take God's place is based on pride and is as old as the rebellion of Satan. It invites God's opposition instead of God's blessing — "God opposes the proud but gives grace to the humble" (James 4:6).

Paradoxically, it is a day when the Lord tells Joshua he will be exalted — "Today I will begin to exalt you in the eyes of all Israel, so they may know that I am with you as I was with Moses" (3:7). This day is going to be a credibility builder for Joshua — people will begin to compare his leadership to that of his predecessor and mentor, Moses. Joshua is to do his part, and let God determine who needs to be "exalted" to move His plan forward.

A concern our staff and lay leaders regularly discuss is that the ministry of our church not center on one person or small group of persons. While leaders need a certain amount of visibility to fulfill their roles in God's movement, that visibility must always be offered to God for His purposes. Our goal is that no one be indispensable except the Head of the Church, Jesus Christ. Any human substitute for the headship of Christ will result in a loss of the staying power necessary for lasting fruit in ministry.

For the Israelites, the focus was not on the obstacles or the human leaders. Their reference point was the ark of the covenant. So should your church go out and purchase an ark? Hardly. What is our reference point to be today? A closer look at what the ark of the covenant represented provides the answer.

First of all, the ark represented the presence of God. It was kept in the Holy of Holies, the most sacred part of the tabernacle where the shekinah glory of God resided. Representations of two angelic beings with wings raised stood on its lid. The "mercy seat" rested beneath the wings (and on top of the ark). God was present and His mercy could be found there.

Secondly, the ark contained the Word of God. Inside were the tablets of stones on which were recorded the Ten Commandments (Hebrews 9:4). These Ten Commandments represented the core values, the non-negotiable authoritative will of God for His people. The ark contained the written word of God and symbolized His authority over His people.

Today, by His Spirit, God resides in us. His Spirit guides us through conviction and affirmation, and "testifies with our spirit that we are God's children" (Romans 8:16). We also have God's written word, the Bible. We give it a place of authority over our tradition, reason and experience. God's Word and God's Spirit provide our reference point. No wonder Jesus tells the woman at the well that "true worshipers will worship the Father in spirit and truth" (John 4:23).

The ark of the covenant helps us not only understand *what* our reference point should be, but *when* we should be especially careful to focus on that reference point. While it's true we should always be sensitive to God's Spirit and responsive to His Word, there are some occasions when we must be strategically focused on God. A quick survey of Joshua reveals how the ark was utilized to bring the Israelites' focus back to their Creator:

- **During new initiatives**. In Joshua 3 and 4 the Israelites are preparing to enter the Promised Land. The territory is unfamiliar to them — "You have never been this way before" (3:4). Because they had never "been there" or "done that," they are to focus on the ark so they will know which way to go. Joshua doesn't allow the people to remain where they are and become completely familiar with the new territory before moving them on. There are some things that cannot be known unless one moves ahead. He points them to something that is familiar to them (the ark) as they enter a land that is unfamiliar (Canaan).

  I've discovered that people don't have to completely grasp the vision or understand all the action plan in order to move forward in God's will. Some things, in fact, cannot be comprehended until after they have been acted upon. The key to moving beyond comfort zones is not knowing all the territory, but being focused on the leadership of God's Spirit.

The launching of a new ministry initiative is a great time for a prayer meeting. It's an opportune time to review the biblical reasons for what is being done.

- **During times of conflict**. In Joshua 6, the Israelites follow the ark of the covenant into battle against Jericho This is one of many times that Scripture records the ark being carried into a conflict. It is a visible reminder of God's presence in the midst of the conflict and of the victory that will ultimately be brought about by God Himself.

A renewed focus on God's Word and Spirit during times of conflict is vital for spiritual leaders. If there is conflict in a marriage, rather than the individual partners focusing on their needs and getting their own ways, they should listen to the inward promptings of the Spirit and see what the Bible says their response should be. If there is emotional turmoil, rather than allowing oneself to be overwhelmed by feelings, focusing on God will help a person receive the peace that transcends understanding. If spiritual warfare is taking place, remember the heavenly armor (Ephesians 6:10-18) designed to equip Christians to overcome the enemy.

The proper focus is also crucial during times of conflict within the church. So many "church fights" are centered on personality clashes or trivial matters. Why do people fight over the color of the carpet or which pew to sit in? Is it because the color scheme or the seating arrangement will influence effectiveness in fulfilling the Great Commission? No, somewhere along the way they've failed to set their hearts and minds on things above (Colossians 3:1-2) and instead have focused on the trivial.

- **During times of failure and confusion**. In Joshua 7, we find Joshua and the elders of Israel falling face down before the ark (7:6). They've just been defeated in battle by the people of Ai in what should have been an easy victory for them. They don't understand why this has happened until God informs them of the sin of Achan that has brought about their downfall.

Failure tends to create a self-centered focus often accompanied by a pity party. "Woe is me" introspection has limited benefit and at times may even cause us to miss what God is saying to us in the aftermath of failure. While I wish I could learn all life's lessons from successful ventures, there are many principles better taught from failure. A soul-searching that seeks God's leading is a way to capitalize on setbacks.

- **During times of worship**. In Joshua 8:30-35, the ark is found in the midst of a public covenant renewal service. Worship services at their best are centered on God's Word and are led by God's Spirit.

Tragically, most public church services are not God-centered. The majority of people leave, asking, "Did that service meet my needs?" not, "What biblical principles did I discover that I can use to honor God this week?" They exit, wondering, "Did that service fulfill my expectations?" instead of, "Did I worship in a way that was responsive to God's Spirit?" Increasingly, worship services are man-centered and must be kept entertaining to satisfy the consumer mentality of most attenders.

Those may be harsh words, and are certainly not meant to excuse poorly planned services or irrelevant messages. I believe a proper focus on God is easier to attain when the service flows according to a biblical theme. When people have prepared thoroughly, they are offering their best to God. But if human preferences are the reference point for worship rather than praise to an awesome God, what we do in church will go no further than the ceiling above our heads.

So how do churches establish God's Word and Spirit as the reference point of their ministries?

1. Be sure that prayer is regularly included in various meetings in the life of the church. Not perfunctory, thoughtless prayers, but those which sincerely invite God's will to be done in that gathering. Don't limit prayer times to the beginning or end of those sessions, but pause spontaneously for prayer.

2. Build worship services around biblical themes such as praise, repentance, obedience or sacrifice. Weave scriptural references into that particular worship service's theme.

3. During decisive moments in your church's history, hold special services that devote time to prayer and relevant Bible study. For instance, on our church's sixteenth anniversary, our evening service was a "concert of prayer" built around the song of Moses recorded in Deuteronomy 32. Moses uses a review of history as an occasion for giving God praise, seeking forgiveness and promising submission to God's will for the future. During our anniversary service we recounted the history of our church. We offered praise, sought forgiveness and committed ourselves to a future that honors God.

4. Bathe any significant change or ministry initiative in prayer. A

consultant employed by churches within our district has wisely counseled that the first item on the agenda of the pastors and lay leaders should be the formation of intercessory prayer groups. He has observed that lasting, spiritually significant changes will not happen unless the Holy Spirit is earnestly sought to create an atmosphere in which they can thrive.

Reverence For God's Powerful Presence

In general, I appreciate the trend toward seeker-sensitivity that is growing in the churches across our nation. Spiritual leaders are becoming more cognizant of the needs of non-churched or de-churched people, and that is helping them build bridges to carry the gospel to non-religious people. Pastors are evaluating the style and content of their messages to see if they are connecting with people who are biblically illiterate but genuine seekers. Local churches as a whole are more active in influencing their various communities rather than withdrawing from them. The danger, however, is in losing perspective. We must always remember that God is our ultimate audience and the One who must be pleased. Losing sight of that focal point leaves a church with a superficial ministry that only caters to the whimsical desires of fickle people and communicates "what their itching ears want to hear" (2 Timothy 4:3).

Our church wrestles with the constant tension between relevance and reverence. We seek to be relevant to our culture, without losing reverence for God. When I was growing up, there were more reminders of the need for reverence. The pastor was referred to as "Reverend"; today our congregation calls me Wayne, or sometimes Pastor Wayne. The room where we held public services was called a "sanctuary"; today we call ours an auditorium. The entryway was once called a "narthex"; now we have a lobby. We're pretty casual and informal, and that's more comfortable for people who aren't used to being in church.

So how do we show our reverence to God? I'm not advocating that people call me Rev. Schmidt (the title currently used only by people who don't know me or are trying to sell me something). I'm not convinced that labeling our rooms with archaic names is the answer. I know many people who use religious sounding titles and labels, and yet show little true reverence for God. I believe Joshua gives us clues as he follows the ark of the covenant in the third chapter of his journal.

- We show reverence for God when we recognize the distance between the Creator (God) and the created (us). Notice the orders the officers give the people: "But keep a distance of about a thousand yards between you and the ark; do not go near it" (3:4). Why should they maintain a space of about ten football fields between them and the ark? To show reverence for God and His holiness. The *distance* points to the *difference* between Creator and creature.

One of the more challenging passages records the death of Uzzah, who is killed for reaching out to steady the ark of the covenant (2 Samuel 6:6-7; 1 Chronicles 13:9-10). Apparently those who were transporting the ark had become careless with it, disregarding God's previous instructions concerning exactly who was to carry it and how it was to be handled. They were treating it like any other piece of luggage — they had become overly familiar with this sacred object.

There is great danger in over-familiarity. I'm grateful for the opportunity to enter God's presence with confidence because of Jesus Christ. I celebrate that I can call out to Him with the words, "Abba, Father." This indicates an intimacy with God that some have said can be captured in the words, "Dear Daddy." He is my Heavenly Father, but He is heavenly . . . and I am earthly.

Many people have reduced God's stature to the point of treating Him as if He's just "one of us." He's our "big buddy." In the words of one song, "We slap God on the back like a buddy from out of town." In the process, many have concluded that God exists to meet our needs, like a genie in a bottle.

Spiritual leaders should model an attitude of submission and reverence for God. In our prayers and in our references to God, it should be obvious that "He is God and we're not." In the process of developing an intimate relationship with Him we must not forfeit our reverence for Him.

- We show reverence for God when we seek our own experience with Him. Joshua tells the people, "Consecrate *yourselves*, for tomorrow the Lord will do amazing things among *you*" (3:5, emphasis added). Joshua wants them to understand that this movement of God is not just about conquering the Promised Land. It is about expanding their vision of God and deepening their commitment to Him.

The same is true for us anytime God does something on our behalf. God is not nearly as interested in changing our circumstances as He is in changing us. He wants us to know Him as the God of the miraculous, the One who does "amazing things," not as just the God of maintenance, the One who does ordinary things. Our consecration is a prerequisite to our own experience with God.

Undoubtedly people have heard and told stories of God's intervention in the lives of their parents and grandparents, but each successive generation must personally encounter the power of God for itself. Christian faith is not a hand-me-down, second-hand experience. Yesterday's experiences with God are not enough for today's generation.

Spiritual leaders must ensure that their young people are encountering the same amazing God they know. This is often thwarted by the false assumption that today's generation will experience God in the same way the previous generations did. We preserve past methods and means rather than focus on the desired outcome — that this generation knows a God who will do "amazing things" among them.

As I mentioned earlier, we have a Saturday night service. It's up tempo (which means there's a band and the music can get boisterous!) and casual (the only suits and ties in the place are worn by visiting ministers checking us out!). When one of our dear older saints decided to visit our Saturday evening service, I warned her that this would not be a "worship" service for her. She insisted she was pretty flexible and it would be fine. Not!

From the expression on her face when she left I knew her flexibility had been stretched and snapped. She said nothing, but the next week I received a letter about the "bar room" atmosphere of the service and the lack of true worshipful music (i.e., hymns).

I generally let a few days pass before I answer letters like these. This gives me time to respond more objectively and allows the letter writer time to receive my response more objectively. But before I could answer her letter, I heard from her again. This time she said, "I realize that service is not for me. I'll stick with our Sunday morning services."

She was right — we designed that service with a particular target audience in mind, and it wasn't for saints in their seventies!

"As I think back on the service," she continued, "while it wasn't what I would consider a worship service, I must admit that the younger people I saw there appeared to be worshipping and genuinely seeking God."

Bravo! She was giving the next generation the opportunity to consecrate themselves to God in a way that was meaningful to them. Reverence means keeping an updated relationship with God. If the last thing God did for you was in the good 'ol days, your relationship with God is a matter of remembrance rather than a matter of reverence.

- We show reverence for God when we see evidence of God at work. "This is how you will know that the *living God is among you*, and that He will certainly drive out before you. . ." the people occupying the land (3:10, emphasis added). They will know God is among them because they will see evidence of Him at work.

  It is an act of worship to look for evidence that God is alive and well. One of the ways we do this is to notice when God answers our prayers and then give Him the credit for it. So often we ask for something from God, He does it, and we move on to our next request as if we are oblivious to what He has done.

  A key dimension of our church's ministry is small groups. This fellowship opportunity is offered nearly every day of the week. Groups meet at a variety of times and in a variety of places. They incorporate into their meetings a time for the sharing of needs and prayer. Many of the groups have taken it a step further. Not only do they make prayer requests, they record those requests in a journal. They review the requests to see if there have been answers to their prayers and then celebrate what God has done. That is an act of reverence — seeing evidence of God at work. It is something that should be a part of the Christian life in times of personal devotions as well as time of public worship. We are irreverent when we take God for granted —- we show reverence when we notice what He has done and thank Him for it. It also reminds us that we serve a God who is alive and well!

- Finally, we show reverence for God when we live in obedience to God's commands. "So when the people broke camp to cross the Jordan, the priests carrying the ark of the covenant went ahead of them" (3:14). When God says "break camp," do we? When He says "move out," do we put it in gear or dig in our heels?

  Obedience is the ultimate test of reverence. No amount of "worship" is a substitute for doing the will of God. King Saul found that out when he disobeyed God and attempted to compensate for it with a hastily convened offering of sacrifices. Samuel confronted him with the words, "To obey is better than sacrifice" (1 Samuel 15:22). The Lord still "detests the sacrifice of the wicked, but the prayer of the upright pleases him" (Proverbs 15:8).

  Do churches sometimes substitute "worship" for obedience? Do they pray earnestly and publicly for lost souls, but make little effort to reach the lost in their community? Do they sing "Faith is the Victory" with gusto, but pursue only risk-free ministry? Do they vigorously discuss passages such as Ephesians 5:29-32, only to leave the room to gossip and let conflicts with others remain unresolved? If they do, their worship shows no reverence for God.

In fact, many people substitute an experience of worship for "moving out" when God tells them to move. They shed a few tears, and feel emotionally relieved — as if that will be an answer for the conviction of God's Spirit they feel. They put a few bucks in the plate as if to bribe God to change His mind. They feel their time in church will be an acceptable trade for the time God wants them to spend influencing their unsaved neighbor. This worship is centered on human comfort, not submission to God.

These are the attitudes and actions of reverence. God is more delighted with these expressions of reverence than with those that are merely a formality.

Our Focal Point

We no longer follow the ark of the covenant, but we are not left to wonder what our ultimate focal point should be:

"Let us *fix our eyes* on Jesus, the author and perfecter of our faith, who for the joy set before him endured the cross, scorning its shame, and sat down at the right hand of the throne of God" (Hebrews 12:2, emphasis added).

Jesus came from heaven to earth, living a life offered in obedience to God's purposes. He is a reference point we can relate to, one who fully entered into our humanity. Yet we owe Him our reverence and allegiance, for He ascended from earth to heaven and has assumed again his rightful place of authority at the throne of God. We set our minds and hearts on things above (Colossians 3:1-2), so that our lives and churches might be available to Him.

Personal Reflection

1. Where did the "focal point" of my life originate? (Possibilities might include God's calling, an unmet need, another person, etc.).

2. Joshua 3:7 tells us that God exalted Joshua. In my times with God, am I humbling myself so that He is free to use me as He pleases?

3. Am I in a time in my life when focusing upon God is particularly important (during new initiatives, times of conflict, times of failure

or confusion, experiences of worship)?

4. Check my attitude during my times of worship. Am I expecting to meet with God? Am I overly critical of those who lead the worship service? Is my focus on my needs alone, or in giving praise to God?

5. Which of the mentioned ways of showing reverence are consistently true of my life? In what other ways can I demonstrate my reverence for God?

6. How instant is my obedience when God speaks? Does God have to try several times to get my attention or build the necessary conviction so I will obey? Am I obedient in all areas, or just some areas?

Inventory for Spiritual Leaders

1. What is the focus of your church's ministry? (Obstacles? Leaders? God?) How do you know this is the focus? Why did you make the choice you did?

2. Is there an inappropriate dependence on any one leader (either pastoral or lay)? It may help to diagnose it by asking questions such as:
   Is there a leader who must be present at every event in the church's life?
   Is there a leader who expects to know every detail of the church's ministry?
   Is there someone the church just "can't get along without" when he or she is gone?

3. What are tangible ways in which you are establishing God's Word and God's Spirit as the reference point for ministry?

4. How up-to-date are your ministries, particularly in reaching the next generation (youth)?

Joshua's Journal:

Lord, prompt me to center my complete life and ministry upon You. Let nothing influence my thoughts, feelings, actions and leadership more than Your Spirit and Word. May I humbly seek You so that You can exalt me to accomplish Your purposes. May our relationship be marked by intimacy, but keep me from ever taking You for granted. Grant me an up-to-date walk with You. Amen.

FOOTNOTES
1. E.C. McKenzie, *Salt and Pepper* (Grand Rapids: Baker Book House, 1974).

Momentum is developed by taking the risk of moving ahead even when significant obstacles remain.

Momentum is drained by succumbing to the "paralysis of analysis."

Chapter Seven

Don't Stop Now

"Once a man understands an idea, he can identify with it, acknowledge it and make it his own."[1]

Aristotle

Joshua's Journal 3

"But one thing I do: Forgetting what is behind and straining toward what is ahead, I press on toward the goal to win the prize for which God has called me heavenward in Christ Jesus. . Join with others in following my example, brothers, and take note of those who live according to the pattern we gave to you" (Philippians 3:13b-14, 17).

Since I am a pastor, people seek my counsel for a variety of reasons. Most often they request guidance in finding God's will for their lives. They may be in a crisis and want to know God's way out. They may be experiencing a significant change and wonder where God wants them to go next.

Knowing God's will is a theologically complex issue, but most times the steps in pursuing it are fairly simple. I frequently lead those I counsel through a series of questions such as:

1. How is your relationship with God?

    The majority of God's will relates to who we are, not what we do. He wants us to walk in fellowship with Him. I'm convinced this is part of the reason God does not drop a "blueprint" of our future from heaven — we'd depend on the blueprint rather than upon Him.

2. Are you living in obedience to God?

    Sin hinders our communication and relationship with God. If we have not done what God has already shown us to do, it's not very likely He'll continue to show us what He has in mind for the future. God is not in the business of satisfying our idle curiosity, or of giving us the whole picture so we can decide whether or not we want to "buy into" His plan.

3. Have you prayed about it?

    This seems like an obvious question, but I'm continually surprised by the number of people who talk to everyone but God about what His will might be for them. Prayer can be hard work, and many detour around it by asking a pastor or a lay leader for advice instead of praying about it themselves.

4. Have you weighed the options?

    Most times, when the above three questions are satisfactorily answered, God expects us to use our "sanctified common sense." He often works through the desires of our hearts and the reasoning of our minds to reveal His direction. Identify the options, and weigh the pros and cons of each option. When this is done prayerfully, it can be a source of great insight.

Once I've reviewed these questions with the people I counsel, I advise them to get moving in a particular direction. I suggest that as they prayerfully move forward, they ask God to close the door if they are headed toward something other than His will. In the words of Henrietta Mears, "You can't steer a parked car." You do the moving; let God do the steering.

I've discovered that when people are experiencing a change, they instinctively slow down. Decision-making has a certain inertia built into it. People can become more committed to protection of self and their interests, opting for the path of least resistance, than to the path that offers the greatest progress. Or they will endlessly review the options before proceeding, allowing the "paralysis of analysis" to take hold.

Part of the task of leadership is to reverse that trend, to create a sense of urgency. Leaders invest their credibility to help people overcome the lethargy that can set in. As leaders help to "get the ball rolling," this momentum gives commitment a chance to flourish. Wise leaders understand the dimensions of momentum, the *process* by which people become part of a movement of God.

That's exactly where we find Joshua and the people as we revisit chapter three of his journal. All the preparations have been made to enter the Promised Land. All that needs to be said has been said, and all that needs to be done has been done. It's time to cross the river. Joshua understands the dynamics of spiritual movement. He doesn't yell, "Everyone into the river!", expecting all to move out at the same time. He orchestrates the transition according to certain principles that are equally relevant to the people of God today.

The Ripple Effect

Ever throw a pebble into the calm waters of a pond? When the pebble hits the water, the ripples begin to radiate from the point of impact. This illustration from the natural realm is a picture of how God works in the spiritual realm.

We're about to witness Joshua's orchestration of the ripple effect. We know that God began this movement in Joshua's heart. It was Joshua who first perceived the change (1:1-2), received the vision (1:3-5) and was challenged to be strong and courageous (1:6-9). He then communicated this to his officers (1:10-18), who went throughout the camp preparing the people to break camp and move out (3:2-4). The priests carrying the ark of the covenant were to lead the processional into the Promised Land (3:6). Representatives from each of the tribes were given a special role in the movement (3:12). Finally, all the people were to join in. Let's diagram that:

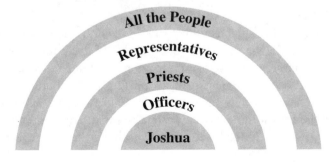

Joshua understands that even though the action being taken is God's will, it's important to align the various sources of influence in such a way that everyone can participate.

This ripple effect is seen in many places. In most businesses, influence ripples from the owner to the managers to the employees. In families, we've all seen the "generational ripple" — from grandparents to parents to children. When the ripple effect transfers godly values and priorities, many people benefit from it. When the created momentum leads in a negative direction, there are adverse consequences for many people. That is why it's important to ask:

1. Whose "ripples" flow into my life? Are those the influences I want to shape my life?

    We are influenced by the people we listen to on the radio, television, computer or in person. We are responsible to God for the things we allow to fill our minds and hearts.

2. Whose lives do my "ripples" impact? Am I being a good steward of the influence I have on others?

    Just as we are to be good stewards of our time, talents and treasure, we are to be faithful stewards of our influence. It is a sacred trust that belongs to God and we need to carefully manage it.

Church leaders are responsible for monitoring not only the impact of their individual influence, but the rippling effect in the church as well.

Building on what is demonstrated in Joshua, we can plot the ripple effect in a local church:

In many churches, just as with Joshua, a vision for ministry begins as God speaks to the heart of an individual. If a church is young, the congregation large, or the pastor has a long tenure of service, most often the vision will begin in the heart of the pastor. If the church is smaller or the pastor is newer, it may be a lay leader who "gets the ball rolling."

Just as the vision moves from Joshua to his officers, so it also moves from the pastor or lay leader to those who have the power to influence.

While I recognize that it's a bit awkward to discuss "power" in the context of a church, it is unwise to ignore the reality of it. There are centers of influence in every congregation. Many a congregation does not make decisions by congregational vote, but by the reaction of a long-term member or generous giver. If that person's head shakes in disapproval, the vision dies. If that person nods in approval, it moves forward. These individuals or families are sometimes called "church bosses" — some use their power very prayerfully and benevolently; others use it selfishly and vindictively. Many churches with dedicated pastors never move ahead because of negative church bosses. To seek their input and support (or at least convince them to remain neutral) can be essential to momentum.

Next the priests join in — those with positions of spiritual leadership in the worship activities of the people. Am I saying that there is a difference between the powerful people and the spiritual people in a congregation? Often it's true that those with the most intimate relationship with God are not necessarily the most influential in the congregation. Sometimes that is for the wrong reasons — less than spiritual people throw their money or weight around. Sometimes it is due to different spiritual gifts — many spiritual people do not have gifts like leadership, administration, and exhortation. They may have gifts like helps or hospitality, which are equally valuable but less visible. But these spiritual people should be sought out to lead the congregation in focusing on the right things as the movement occurs. Just as the priests were to carry the ark of the covenant, so these people are characterized by a reverence for God that is the hallmark of any eternally significant movement.

Then the representatives of the various tribes are given a part in the process. Likewise churches, especially those that are larger, have various "tribes" (interest groups). These may be leaders that minister to a particular age group, such as children, youth or seniors. They may be leaders of classes or small groups. Congregations are often not one big family, but a gathering of various sub-groups. Attaining ownership of the vision from representatives of various "tribes" helps build momentum.

Finally, all the people join in. Tragically, this is where many pastors or leaders start. They sense a vision from God, then stand in front of the church in a worship service or congregational meeting and "announce" the will of God for the people. Human nature being what it is, the initial response will usually be resistance. The people feel the leader has sprung something on them and they've had no part in the process. The leader concludes the people aren't interested in "God's vision" and aren't responsive to the leading of God's Spirit. The problem may not be with the vision or the people at all, but with the *process*. The ripple effect has been ignored.

What are some key dimensions to orchestrating a ripple effect in the local church?

1. **Seek God's will.** Be certain that the ripple effect isn't being employed for selfish or wrong reasons. The process of momentum degenerates into a process of manipulation if God's Spirit is not in it.

2. **Identify those who need to be part of the process.** Who has influence? Who will maintain a godly focus throughout the transition? Have representatives from various groups been included? Most church leaders, with some intentional consideration, can identify these people.

3. **Don't underestimate the need for redundant communication.** This means presenting the idea many times and in many ways. Just as ripples in a pond tend to dissipate as they move out from the point of initiation, so a vision blurs as it goes through the process of transmission.

4. **Make room for several "ripple creators."** I serve with several other pastors on our church staff who are very capable of "getting the ball rolling" in their areas of ministry. Sometimes there are "white caps" when ripples collide, making for rough water! But under the umbrella of a common larger vision, there is room in a growing congregation for many initiating leaders. Many pastors or lay leaders limit momentum because they wrongfully conclude they should only support what they have originated.

5. **Consider the many different ripple effects in the life of a church.** We're all aware of the negative ones — a prominent member who falls into sin, a family that breaks up, or a gossip who spreads rumors. However, there are also different types of positive and necessary ripples:

   • Fundraising is often strengthened through the ripple effect. Many financial campaigns are designed with initial commitments from the staff, board, key lay leaders and givers before the congregation at large registers its commitments. The congregation is encouraged by these leadership gifts.

   • Spiritual revival can be precipitated as God moves first in the hearts of a few, then others, and finally the whole congregation. A sense of anticipation in worship can build as people share with the congregation what God has done for them and what they believe He wants to do for the total church.

- Outreach efforts such as "Friend Day" can benefit from the ripple effect. Many of the most successful "Friend Days" have begun by the pastor mentioning the friend he's invited, then board members announcing the friends they've invited, then key lay leaders announcing the friends they've invited. This gives the congregation a chance to accept the idea and consider those they may want to invite.

These are but a few of the areas where healthy churches experience the ripple effect.

Spiritual leaders must participate in this process. Neutrality is a myth — a leader must exercise appropriate stewardship of influence without developing a spirit of pride. There is no greater joy than fulfilling one's role in a movement of God!

The Threshold

Between the people of God and the land God has promised them flows the Jordan River. The time has come for the leaders to step in, and as soon as their feet touch the water's edge, Joshua predicts the waters will part:

"And as soon as the priests who carry the ark of the Lord — the Lord of all the earth — *set foot in the Jordan*, its waters flowing downstream will be cut off and stand up in a heap" (3:13, emphasis added).

What Joshua predicts comes true as the people of God move out. "Yet as soon as the priests who carried the ark reached the Jordan and their feet touched the water's edge, the water from upstream stopped flowing" (3:15-16). The miracle was dependent upon their willingness to step in and cross the threshold.

Between every promise of God and its fulfillment lies a "river" that will test the faith of spiritual leaders. It is an obstacle to overcome. And obstacles cause people to balk.

There are multitudes of people who know where they are in life and also know what God has promised them. But they are stuck at the edge of the river — unwilling to step in. Lots of tremendous people are mediocre Christians because they lack the willingness and faith to cross the threshold. It is the difference between knowing what decision to make and having the courage to make that decision.

In the same way, many churches go only to the river's edge and no farther. It's not that they don't know the promises of God — in fact, these churches may be full of people who pray fervently and study Scripture diligently. But they are intimidated by the threshold — whether it be financial, organizational, or spiritual. So inertia sets in, the years go by, and the ministry dies a slow death.

Over the years our church has encountered many such thresholds. During these times, the "simple" growth everyone enjoys is replaced by what distinguishes the truly committed — "sacrificial" growth. In broad strokes, I trace our church's history in this way:

"Sacrificial growth": During these years (1979-1983), we met in rented facilities with no guarantees that our new church would survive. The inconveniences and challenges ensured that everyone who joined with us did so because they believed in our vision and had faith in our future. Numerical growth, however, was very slow during this time.

"Simple growth": We moved into our first new facility, and people joined us by the hundreds. Some came because they believed in the vision, some because of the programs, some because they liked our new little church building. For the first time we had a significant number of people who were just spectators, who did nothing more than attend. Growth was simple in this time period (1983-1985), not requiring much commitment from those who attended. It was easy to be part of the church during this time.

"Sacrificial growth": We began the process of relocation from our 6.4 acre site to our 50 acre site. This transition period (1986-1987) fostered a new level of expectation for financial and ministry involvement. Some people left, feeling they were losing the church they had "simply" been enjoying. For those who remained, however, there was greater ownership in the vision and a blossoming of new levels of commitments.

"Simple growth": Relocation complete, we overcame the initial discomfort of being in new facilities. During this period (1987-1992) we grew rapidly in attendance and had new visibility in our community. People wanted to be part of the church where things were "happening" and momentum was building. It was "simple" to enjoy what God was doing and to slip in and slip out of services.

"Sacrificial growth": We began discussing a new sanctuary project and raising funds for it (1992-1996), but have not yet moved in. The size of the facility and the finances it necessitates tests our commitment to reach our community for Christ. Again people have left and attendance growth has plateaued. People are counting the cost of being part of the church's future and determining whether they are willing to sacrifice personally to invest in it.

While there have been other thresholds along the way, these are the major defining moments in our church's history. If you were to plot your church's history according to periods of "simple" growth and "sacrificial" growth, how would it look? If you were to plot your personal spiritual history, where would you see the thresholds of commitment?

Here are some observations from those times at the "river's edge," those moments that require faith to step in and take a risk in order to be part of what God is doing:

1. Many people will come during times of "simple" growth, just as Jesus was followed by great crowds who witnessed His miracles and listened to His parables. But their level of commitment is not known until the church enters a period of "sacrificial" growth.

2. Because people do not stay with a church during a "sacrificial" time does not mean they are less spiritual or less committed. Although that may be true for some, it may also be that for the first time others are grasping the church's vision and don't feel "led of God" to be part of it. When sacrifice is required people become more thoughtful about the future and whether that future is one they will choose. Be careful about speaking in derogatory terms about those who leave — departure may be God's will for them.

3. People who leave during a "sacrificial" time may return when the "simple" growth phase returns. For instance, some people who left us when we were anticipating relocation returned after relocation was complete. They watched things happen rather than take part in the happening.

4. Sometimes people are uncomfortable with a threshold the church is crossing because they are simultaneously crossing a personal threshold. They may be overwhelmed with a family situation or career transition. They may have all they can do to cross that threshold, let alone be part of the move the church is making.

5. Spiritual life and character are deepened during the "sacrificial" growth, not the "simple" growth periods. That is true of individuals and of churches. It is sacrifice that tests the fiber of a pastor, lay leader or congregation. It's amazing (and disappointing) how many pastors feel "called of God" to move elsewhere when they sense that simple growth is ending and sacrifice lies just ahead. Lay people sense that same "call." This leaves churches on plateaus and people in shallow walks of faith.

Crossing a threshold requires faith, and Joshua demonstrates the courageous faith necessary to move forward. This section in his journal reveals two stages of faith:

The "Say It" stage - Joshua announces what God will do (3:13) before God performs the miracle. Joshua has the courage to hear from God and then communicate the promises of God to His people. It takes courage to publicly commit to a future you believe God has provided before other people witness God at work.

The "Step In" stage - The hearers take action on what has been heard and communicated. All that needs to be said has been said — it's time for faith to go to work.

The threshold involves risk and the investment of Joshua's credibility as a leader. Once the threshold is crossed, however, his credibility is greater than ever before. God exalts him in the eyes of the people, "so they may know that I am with you as I was with Moses" (3:7).

A threshold is a defining moment. It separates those who are excited about the concept from those who will embrace the commitment. When was the last time you got your feet wet? When was the last time your church "stepped in" to a significant test of faith?

The Adoption Curve

Spiritual leaders are crucial to the *start up* of a movement of God, so their ripples of influence encourage others. They also take the lead in *stepping in* when there is a threshold of commitment to be crossed. But there is another dimension of momentum — *standing firm* until the test of faith passes:

"The priests who carried the ark of the covenant of the Lord *stood firm* on dry ground in the middle of the Jordan, while all Israel passed by until the whole nation had completed the crossing on dry ground" (3:17, emphasis added).

The steadiness of the priests must have encouraged those whose faith wavered as they crossed the river.

Undoubtedly the people passing through had their doubts and concerns. Some were probably thinking, "With my luck, as soon as I step in the river bed the wall of water will give way." The next chapter of Joshua gives us a humorous glimpse of their apprehension:

"Now the priests who carried the ark remained standing in the middle of the Jordan until everything the Lord had commanded Joshua was done by the people, just as Moses had directed Joshua. The people *hurried over*, and as soon as all of them had crossed . . ." (4:10-11, emphasis added).

I can picture the people walking slowly to the water's edge, almost dragging their feet. Then they make a mad dash across the river bed! Once on the other side, they probably slowed their pace again and acted as if crossing the river was no big deal! Like many of us today, the Israelites were willing to cross the threshold but they sure weren't going to linger there!

The priests stood firm. I believe some people who crossed the river that day did not have great faith in God. They might not even have been excited about the Promised Land — the desert was just fine for them! They had the courage and willingness to cross the river, however, because when their faith wavered (or maybe had not yet even developed), they saw their spiritual leaders standing firm.

Years ago, while doing doctoral studies on change management, I first came across a formidable field of research on "the diffusion of innovation." Fortunately, its basic premise has been reduced to simpler form and has become popularly known as the "adoption curve." The adoption curve validates something we all have observed. Some people are more open to change than others. Some welcome change, even get restless when it is not taking place. Others — being committed to the status quo — resist change. In churches, people are located at various points on this change continuum:

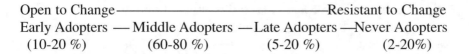

Open to Change———————————————————Resistant to Change
Early Adopters — Middle Adopters —Late Adopters —Never Adopters
  (10-20 %)   (60-80 %)   (5-20 %)   (2-20%)

Aubrey Malphurs and others give us some additional insights into these groups:

1. Early Adopters generally make up 10-20% of a congregation. Their motto is "believing is seeing" and they adopt new ideas quickly. They not only are open to change, but get restless if some changes aren't happening. They may even create change for change's sake in situations where it is not warranted.

2. Middle Adopters make up the majority of most churches (60-80%). Not quick to accept new ideas, they initially offer resistance. However, once they have time to think about a worthwhile change, and see the commitment of others to it, they hop on the band wagon and actively support the initiative.

3. Late Adopters comprise normally 5-20% of a local church. They resist change, holding to the motto "seeing is believing." Only after the vast majority of people has actively embraced the change are they willing to go along. Even then, they may simply acquiesce to what is happening and lobby for a return to "the way things were" if the change process stumbles.

4. Never Adopters (2-20%) will not embrace the change no matter who is for it and how worthwhile it turns out to be. They'll drag their feet into eternity — committed to the past and backing into the future.[2]

As I've looked at our church and briefly glimpsed the experience of other churches, I've made these observations:

- The longer a church has been around and the longer it has been since changes have been made, the more the church membership is found on the right side of the continuum. There are more middle and late adopters — fewer early adopters. Conversely, the newer a church is, or the more frequently it has experienced change, the more the church membership is found on the left side of the continuum. This is part of the reason newer churches are more flexible than older churches.

- Which types of adopters are selected for leadership says a lot about a church. Churches longing for stability resist placing early adopters in places of influence, while churches aiming for increased creativity and flexibility often seek out early adopters as leaders.

- How open a person is to change is more a reflection of experience and personality than of spiritual maturity. Leaders must resist the tendency to label certain people as spiritual or carnal based on their response to change.

- Church leaders tend to spend too much of their time with "never adopters," who are often the proverbial squeaky wheels that get the oil. To prepare a church for the future it is a much better stewardship of time to invest in early and middle adopters.

Recognizing the various responses to change will help your church strategically involve as many as possible in a movement of God.

How does this relate to "standing firm"? I believe standing firm allows more people to be part of what God is doing. The middle adopters — and even to some extent the late adopters — will become part of the change by witnessing the unwavering commitment of others to it. The faithfulness and consistency of spiritual leaders as times passes allows more people to "hop on the bandwagon" and acquire ownership of the vision.

Anyone who has been a spiritual leader knows that transition times make people nervous. People will seek leaders out to discover whether or not they are really committed to the new direction. If the leaders waver in their commitment, people may refuse to accept the change. If the leaders are consistent in their commitment, the people's nervousness begins to dissipate and resistance fades. People are watching — and a spiritual leader's firm stand helps them take new steps of faith.

Personal Reflection

1. If I am currently seeking God's will, what will my answers be to these questions:
   How is my relationship with God?
   Am I living in obedience to God?
   Have I prayed about it?
   Have I weighed the options?

2. Whose ripples of influence consistently flow into my life? Is this the influence I desire in order to develop my spiritual life and ministry?

3. Who is affected by the ripples of my influence? Am I a good steward of the influence God has entrusted to me?

4. Plot my own personal spiritual history based on the phases of

"sacrificial" growth and "simple" growth. Be sure to identify the "defining moments" that occur along the way.

5. How open to change am I? What kind of "adopter" am I most naturally inclined to be? Is this an asset or liability in my spiritual life?

Inventory for Spiritual Leaders

1. Can you envision the ripple effect that occurs in your church? Who are the "power" people? The "spiritual" people? The representatives of key groups?

2. Do you attempt to orchestrate the ripple effect in your church? Can you identify a time when you've seen the ripple effect work negatively? Positively?

3. Plot your church's history based on the "simple" growth and "sacrificial" growth scenario. What period are you in now?

4. What have been some of the defining moments (either negative or positive) in your church's history?

5. How would you rate your congregation's openness to change? In other words, what percentage of your congregation would you place in each of the adopter categories?

Joshua's Journal

Lord, I will seek your will and commit to it even when sacrifices are involved. Help me to be a good steward of the influence that You have entrusted to me. Help me to continue to stand firm in your plans even when others waver. Keep me open to change — not just for change's sake, but for your sake, O Lord. Amen.

FOOTNOTES
1. Leith Anderson, *Dying For Change* (Minneapolis: Bethany House Publishers, 1990), p. 179.
2. Aubrey Malphurs, *Pouring New Wine Into Old Wineskins* (Grand Rapids: Baker Books, 1993), pp. 100-106.

Momentum is developed by seeking to leave a lasting legacy that is a witness for years to come.

Momentum is drained by settling for superficial success or being satisfied to worship what God has done in the past.

Chapter Eight

A Legacy Worth Following

"May all who come behind us find us faithful. May the fire of our devotion light their way."[1]

Jon Mohr

Joshua 4

"This is what Hezekiah did throughout Judah, doing what was good and right and faithful before the Lord his God. In everything that he undertook in the service of God's temple and in obedience to the law and the commands, he sought his God and worked wholeheartedly. And so he prospered" (2 Chronicles 31:20-21).

Measuring success is a baffling exercise. It seems everyone has a different perspective on what represents a "successful" person or organization. Christian leaders find it even more complicated, for the ultimate criteria is not found in the realm of man but in the eternal judgments and rewards of God.

There are a variety of factors that influence how a leader evaluates success:

- **A person's history**

   Upbringing and past experiences influence one's view of success. Many adults still live to please their parents, and will not feel successful until their parents are satisfied. Many church leaders compare their present church with the one in which they were raised or the church they first attended after their commitment to Christ. They determine success through a historical reference point.

   This means of evaluating success is less than objective, because a person's view of history is frequently more a matter of perception than reality. How we *remember* the past often overrides the actuality of the past. As a general rule, if people feel positive about a past experience, they tend to exaggerate its good. If they feel negative about a past experience, they tend to magnify the bad.

   I've been amazed at the gap that exists between perception and reality. Because our congregation is a melting pot of church backgrounds, people at times prompt our church to conform to methods used by a church they've previously attended. Some of these souls who come to our church because "we're different from what they are used to" will, after a period of time, begin to long for the good old days, attempting to change our church to reflect their past! One couple shared with me, for instance, how great the small group ministry was in their previous church. Being one who seeks to learn from others, I called their former church to learn about this great small group ministry. I discovered that it's very similar to ours — but they perceive a world of difference. It is perception, not reality, that influences feelings.

- **Personality**.

   Someone with a competitive personality measures success by outperforming another person. Someone who is cooperative associates success with being a team player. A dominant person views success as being able to have everything under control. A highly relational person feels successful when everyone else feels good about what has been accomplished.

   Our ministry seeks to help our leaders identify their spiritual gifts. We've also attempted to assist them in understanding their personality styles. One year all church board members completed a personality profile. We began to laugh when we realized how often our personalities reflected our positions on issues. We also recognized that while the ability to be truly objective in a discussion is impossible, discussion is usually enhanced when people are cognizant of the natural tendencies of their personalities.

- **Peer group**

    It is human nature to compare ourselves with people we view as peers. If we are keeping pace with them, or doing a bit better than they are, we feel successful. If we're losing ground, we may become anxious and conclude that we've failed.

    While I'd like to believe that spiritual leaders never engage in harmful comparison, it is a regular activity in ministerial gatherings and denominational conferences. I've witnessed people who have had a great year of ministry deflate after someone details a year that appears even better. I've witnessed leaders who should repent for their ineffectiveness in ministry console themselves by finding other leaders even less disciplined! The Apostle Paul warns of the danger of comparison (2 Corinthians 10:12). Scripture emphasizes that each of us must give an account (Hebrews 4:13).

Factors like these make "success" a highly subjective phenomenon.

Churches try to evaluate their success, and should. As I've interacted with pastors and leaders of many churches, I've observed a continuum of success measurement:

Superficial --- Spiritualized

While few church leaders are found at the extreme ends of the spectrum, let me briefly describe how those ends might appear.

Superficial

In this category, external measurements are the only ones that are necessary. A sense of success rises and falls with the attendance pattern. It inflates with the growth of buildings or budgets. It can be associated with the number of prestigious people who attend the church, or with those who have gone out from the church and made an impact in their careers or ministry.

There are many problems in using this category to measure a church's success. For instance, external standards of measurement keep changing. When I was growing up, success was a matter of how many buses the church owned. There was no such thing as small groups. Now few people talk about their buses, but many talk about the number of small groups in their church. In The Wesleyan denomination, a church with an attendance or membership of 500 used to be considered a mega-church. Now our denomination has several churches that exceed that number in worship attendance. Success is a moving target.

But there are even more serious problems with superficial, external measurements. Attendance growth may be a symptom of novelty rather than ministry. Church budgets may expand by catering to wealthy donors, but result in the compromise of biblical standards. Excessive building programs may drain dollars and attention from much more worthy endeavors.

A few years ago I visited a church in Birmingham, Alabama. It advertised a sanctuary that seated ten thousand people. It was beautiful from the road, but as we pulled into the parking lot, the signs of disrepair were obvious. Entering the facility, we noticed that poor maintenance had resulted in a facility that looked several years older than its actual age. We met with the pastor who explained that he was ministering with a very limited staff and program due to budget constraints.

As his story unfolded, we learned that a previous pastor's "vision from God" had dictated the building of a huge sanctuary. This vision severely strained the church's financial resources. The resulting pressure, along with construction difficulties, resulted in a church split. The pastor left to form a new church down the road with people who were willing to believe in the vision "God had given him." Now the new pastor was enthusiastically leading a struggling congregation to rebuild its ministry in the face of incredible obstacles. That big sanctuary, rather that being a symbol of success, had led to the downfall of that church's mission.

Spiritualized

People on this end of the "success" continuum resist any external, tangible assessments of accomplishment. It is hard to criticize this approach, because on the surface it sounds so spiritual. It is difficult to argue with such pious platitudes as:

"God has simply called us to be faithful."
"If it reaches just one soul, it's worth it."
"We may be small, but we are spiritual."
"It's quality that matters to God, not quantity."

There is an element of spiritual truth in each of these sayings. God does value faithfulness in the lives of His people and churches. Jesus Himself told the story of one lost sheep (Luke 15:1-7), highlighting the worth of one soul. Christ's ministry often took Him away from the crowds, allowing Him to spend time with a few who were committed to following Him.

However, when a "small but spiritual" church fails to win one person to Christ in a year's time, someone has to ask some tough questions about whether that church is responding in obedience to the Great Commission. If church budgets are stagnant, the question of whether there has been an appropriate challenge to biblical stewardship should be addressed. If attendance is declining while the surrounding community is growing, where is the "salt and light" of spiritual influence?

Joshua's journal helps us evaluate success from God's perspective. We see in chapter 4 the initial fulfillment of a promise God gave Joshua earlier:

> "Be strong and very courageous. Be careful to obey all the law my servant Moses gave you; do not turn from it to the right or to the left, that you may be **successful** wherever you go. Do not let this Book of the Law depart from your mouth; meditate on it day and night, so that you may be careful to do everything written in it. Then you will be prosperous and **successful**" (Joshua 1:7-8, emphasis added).

Now they have entered the Promised Land, completing the first successful steps in a series of acts of obedience that will lead them to conquer this new territory. Their first instructions from God in the Promised Land lead them to construct what I call a "success symbol," a memorial to a miracle.

God's Success Symbol

When the whole nation has crossed the Jordan, God commands Joshua to construct a monument. God gives detailed plans for its creation (4:2-3). Joshua passes those instructions on to the twelve representatives from the twelve tribes of Israel (4:4-7). The representatives carry out the instructions they receive from God through Joshua (4:8-9).

A closer look at the symbol gives us insight into what it represents. It consists of twelve stones, one for each of the twelve tribes of Israel. The stones stand for the unity of the nation of Israel and the participation of everyone in the miracle God had done.

The stones are taken from the middle of the Jordan where the priests had firmly stood with the ark of the covenant. When the people passed by, the ark of the covenant represented God's promises. Selecting the stones from this location would remind people of the miraculous presence of God. So this symbol of success highlights the participation of all of the people and God's provision for them.

What symbols remind Christians of similar truths today? Certainly there is the *cross*, reminding us of the successful completion of Christ's mission to the world. God's love and the sacrifice of His Son give all people the opportunity to enter into a right relationship with God.

There is the celebration of *baptism*, a public act of commitment that symbolizes dying to the worldly self and being raised to new life in Christ.

The practice of *communion* symbolizes the substitution of Christ as an offering for our sin. The bread represents His body broken for us; the cup, His blood shed for us. At His command we receive the elements in remembrance of Him.

Symbols are powerful reminders, but they can present problems to Christians. Sometimes people forget the meaning of the symbol, or attach the wrong meaning to it. People may worship the symbol rather than the action of God which the symbol represents.

Symbols can also cause an inappropriate focus on the past. It is much easier to worship a past movement of God than it is to invest the credibility and energy necessary to be part of a new movement of God!

But when symbols are used appropriately, they help us recall God's faithfulness in providing what we need to live in a way that honors Him. The symbol God instructs Joshua to create points to the true measurements of success. These measurements remain valid today in determining the success of a movement of God.

Measurement # 1 - Transitions in Obedience to God

The symbol pointed to the successful completion of a transition that had been God's will for decades. The Israelites had crossed the threshold of the Jordan River, leaving behind a life of desert wandering and embarking on the conquest of new territory for God. They had exercised faith in God and carried out His instructions.

Although transition times can be difficult, making it through them is cause for celebration. It is important to recall defining moments — those times when we knew what God wanted us to do and we did it; and when, because of our willingness and His power, new opportunities were given.

In 1987 our church relocated to its present property. We had constructed a multi-use facility with a balance of space for children, youth and adults. Our rapid growth following that move meant the addition of worship services and educational hours. All age groups felt the strain, but none more greatly than our children and youth.

Because we were still in debt from the relocation, we believed it was impossible to add facilities through additional borrowing. So we constructed facilities to serve our children and youth, raising the necessary funds through a campaign called "To Kids . . .With Love." When we completed this educational wing debt-free, we wanted to acknowledge the generous giving and substantial sacrifice of our people. We also wanted to keep the focus on our children. Our solution was to hang a display entitled "To Kids. . .With Love" in the facility. The display contains the names of the children who motivated us to give, not the donors who actually gave. Every time our children are in the building, they see their names engraved in this display — it is a symbol of our congregation's love and commitment to them.

That display is also a symbol of a threshold of commitment for our congregation. At a time when many had already given generously, we stepped up to the challenge and God miraculously provided. That transition time resulted in more than a building. It resulted in a whole new opportunity to impact the lives of children for Christ.

Measurement # 2 - Involvement of God's People

The twelve stones represented the participation of the twelve tribes of Israel in crossing the Jordan River. The crossing was something the whole nation did together, even though two-and-a-half tribes would later return to the other side of the Jordan to live. It utilized everyone's abilities — the officers with their military strategy, the priests with their spiritual ministry, the people who prepared to move the camp into the Promised Land. Everyone *celebrated* what God had done because everyone *participated* in what God had done.

The finest successes are those which involve the whole body of Christ getting in on the action. Consider the words of 1 Corinthians 12:14, "The body is not made up of one part but of many." None of us is exempt from being a part of what God is doing (12:15-20). All of us need each other; we are not self-sufficient and we do not individually possess all of God's spiritual gifts (12:21-27).

Spiritual leaders must ensure that they help people discover their spiritual gifts and provide opportunities for the use of them. In some churches, people are left with the impression that they don't have a ministry unless they can teach or sing. But what about the gifts of helps and service? Are gifts of mercy and giving being utilized? Leadership and administration? Is there a way to involve every person and his or her gifts in a church-wide emphasis?

From the beginning, our church has sought to help people discover their spiritual gifts and then to pursue a ministry which utilizes those gifts. Early on, this was accomplished through a program I designed called "B.E.A.M. — Believers Enabled As Ministers." Today we use some of the newer, more sophisticated programs now available. At times we've done a very good job of helping people identify their gifts and involving them in ministry, and those were times when our church seemed especially vibrant. At other times we've become busy and fallen into the "it's-easier-to-do-it myself" mentality. When people begin to stand on the sidelines as spectators, it's natural for them to become critical and feel as if they don't belong. That slowly drains the vitality from a church.

Measurement # 3 - Credibility of the Leaders

True success grants spiritual leaders even greater influence in the lives of their people. Joshua had long been in the shadow of his predecessor Moses, but the successful crossing of the Jordan River and entry into the Promised Land gives new credibility to Joshua's leadership: "That day the Lord exalted Joshua in the sight of all Israel; and they revered him all the days of his life, just as they had revered Moses" (4:14). Joshua has been strong and courageous in fulfilling his role to move the people of God forward, so God exalts him.

In any movement of God there must be leaders who are willing to humbly risk or invest their credibility. This is an act which serves God's people and gives glory to God. Leaders who are proud focus on what their actions will do for them; those who are humble are more concerned about what their actions will accomplish for God and others. When God sees a spiritual leader humbly but courageously risk personal credibility, He knows He can trust that leader with additional influence. "The greatest among you will be your servant. For whoever exalts himself will be humbled, and whoever humbles himself will be exalted" (Matthew 23:11-12). Joshua's goal was not to be revered like Moses. If it had been, God would probably not have used him. Joshua's goal was to be a faithful leader and let God take care of the rest.

Sometimes leaders claim success, but a closer look reveals that it has come at the expense of their respect in the eyes of others. This is not to say that people will always agree with the leader's direction, or that they won't ask some tough questions along the way. In fact, between the leader's initial investment of his existing credibility and the gift from God of additional credibility, there is often a period of uncertainty. So, in a way, a measurement of success can't be applied until the movement is completed. As the people look back, do they have greater respect for the leader as someone who courageously obeys God, or less respect for the leader as someone who pridefully does what he wants?

Measurement # 4 - Spiritual Legacy to Those who Follow

The finest success symbols are those which transform physical, programmatic victories into spiritual legacies. The people had crossed the Jordan River and entered the Promised Land — that was a physical, historical event. The monument reminded them that the event was a miracle of God: God provides a way for His people to experience what He has promised. That pile of stones would remain a part of their spiritual legacy.

God knew the stones would serve as a sign among His people for generations to come. The monument would prompt future generations to ask, "What do these stones mean?" (4:6, 21). It would create teachable moments for emphasizing such things as how the "flow of the Jordan was cut off before the ark of the covenant of the Lord" (4:6) and, "The Lord your God did to the Jordan just what he had done to the Red Sea when he dried it up before us until we had crossed over" (4:23).

Several years ago, the church I attended while growing up conducted a financial campaign. My parents, who were still members of that church, believed that building a new sanctuary was absolutely necessary to the future outreach of the church. When the time arrived for financial commitments, they put their treasure where their hearts were — they gave generously.

Because they had arrived at their decision prayerfully and had taken a significant step of faith with their financial pledge, they were asked to share their testimony with others. My dad, a man of relatively few words, spoke from his heart. While I was not there personally, others reported to me that he mentioned the pledge might have an impact on their children's inheritance. He felt, however, that the most important thing he could leave his children was not a few more dollars, but a "legacy of generosity." He wanted us to know that financial blessings come from God, and that God should be generously honored with them. By their actions, my parents took a physical victory (success in business) and created a spiritual legacy.

Every once in a while, in my more sentimental moments, I drive through my old neighborhood and pull into the parking lot of my former church. My parents no longer attend there — my dad worships God with the angels in heaven. My widowed mother has moved and now attends the church I pastor. Even though my parents no longer attend the old church, every time I see that sanctuary, do you know what comes to my mind? Those words — "legacy of generosity." That building is a sign to me of God's faithfulness to my parents and their faithfulness to Him.

Measurement # 5 - Testimony to Those Yet to Know God

Many people have mistakenly concluded after reading the Old Testament that God was only interested in His chosen people, the nation of Israel. It is true that God selected them from all the peoples of the earth to demonstrate His love and power. However, His work on their behalf was to be a testimony to the whole world of the benefits of submitting to God and seeking a relationship with Him. God placed Israel on center stage, but He knew the world was watching and deciding whether they, too, would follow Him. That is evident in the miracle of crossing the Jordan River as well. God was not only interested in doing something for His own people but, "He did this so that all the peoples of the earth might know . . ." (4:24). Perhaps some would put their faith in Him as Rahab did. Others would continue in their allegiance to false gods and resist the living God.

The "success symbol" not only carried a message for God's people and the generations that followed them, but for all the peoples of the earth. A movement of God is successful when it not only blesses and builds the faith of those who already belong to Him, but witnesses to those who have yet to know and trust Him.

As I mentioned earlier, we are in the process of constructing a new sanctuary. In a sense, that new building is nothing more than a stack of stones. This is not meant to offend the architects who designed it — (for what it costs, it better look like more than a stack of stones!). Neither is it meant to downplay how functional it will be or how valuable a tool it will be for ministry. But like the stack of twelve stones in Joshua, it has something to say to subsequent generations. We hope when our children ask, "What do these stones mean?" that it says to them, "The most important activity in the world is the worship of God." God is worthy of our worship.

But we also pray that those in our surrounding community will ask, "What do these stones mean?" Even if they have yet to commit their lives to God, we hope the facility will say, "Our church family is making room for you." We hope it says, "Experiencing God's presence and hearing God's truth is what growing numbers of people should experience." Ultimately we hope it means, "God is worthy of the worship of every person in this community and every person on the face of this earth." We're already praying that the facility, upon completion, will be a testimony to "the peoples of the earth."

Measurement # 6 - Reminder of the Power of God

The success Joshua and Israel experienced pointed to the power of

God. "He did this so that all the peoples of the earth might know that the hand of the Lord is **powerful** and so that you might always fear the Lord your God" (14:24, emphasis added). Success points to the activity and sovereignty of God. If the only conclusion had been that Joshua was a great leader or the people had accomplished something special, it would have fallen short of lasting success.

When the power of God is experienced, it is evidenced by increased obedience on the part of His people. It builds their *fear* of the Lord, an awesome respect for what God can do. The result is submission to God which is preparation for what He wants to do through them next. False success says, "Look at what we have done," and rests on the laurels of past accomplishment. True success points to the reality that "the hand of the Lord is powerful" and that we should "always fear the Lord." That prepares us for the next chapter of His plan.

Joshua's Summary of Success

1. Change is inevitable and times of transition will come. Courageous obedience to the prompting of God creates new challenges and opens new doors of opportunity.

2. God has a role for every person in His mission. There are a variety of roles, so He has given a diversity of gifts. Leaders plan for everyone to participate, and no person settles for being just a spectator.

3. There will be times of tension — even suffering — for spiritual leaders. It is impossible to please everyone. However, if the exercise of a person's leadership is graced with humility and integrity, that leader will have greater respect and credibility in the eyes of his or her followers.

4. Leaders must continually connect the progress that is achieved with the provision of God. Organizational victories must be transformed into spiritual legacies by constantly raising people's awareness of God's involvement in them.

5. God is a missionary. He seeks to receive the worship of every person He has created, drawing them from every community and country in the world. Leaders help their followers transcend the natural tendency to become ingrown and elevate their own needs above the needs of others.

6. Ultimately, spiritual leadership heightens people's awareness of an

awesome God. This awareness leads them to consistently make those changes which transform their individual lives and give fresh momentum to a movement of God.

Personal Reflection

1. By what criteria do I evaluate my personal success? Is this the criteria I want to continue to use in the future?

2. Have I identified my spiritual gifts? Am I actively functioning in the Body of Christ by serving Him and others with my gifts?

3. What kind of legacy am I leaving behind? If a eulogy is given at my funeral, what will be mentioned?

4. Have I formulated my testimony of faith in Jesus Christ so that it can be communicated to others?

5. Additional reading: *Soul Management* by Wayne Schmidt.[2]

Inventory for Spiritual Leaders

1. In what ways do you evaluate the success of your church? How do you measure the success of the pastor? The church board? Other lay leaders?

2. Have you provided a means for people in your church to discover their spiritual gifts? Are there ministry roles available to utilize a variety of gifts?

3. What is the reputation and impact of your church in the surrounding community?

Joshua's Journal

Lord, may I invest my life in those things which lead to lasting success. May I measure the significance of my life in spiritual terms, no superficial terms. May the legacy I leave not point people to me, bu point people to You. Amen.

FOOTNOTES
1. Jon Mohr, from the song "Find Us Faithful." Birdwing Music/Jonathon Mark Music, 1987.
2. Wayne Schmidt, *Soul Management* (Grand Rapids: Zondervan Publishing, 1996).

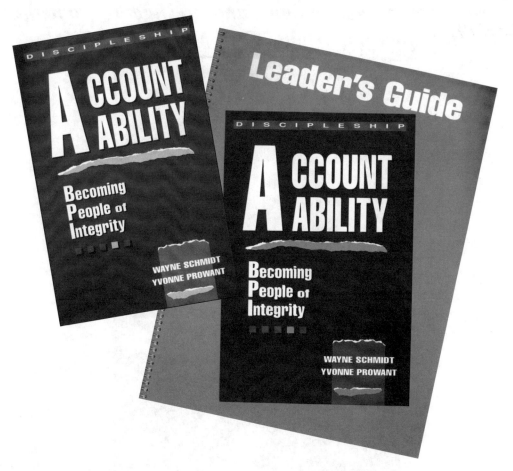

Accountability—Becoming People of Integrity is designed to be a "how-to" book, written to more adequately equip people to implement personal accountability. You will learn the biblical basis for accountability and how to determine values, goals, and priorities that will help you keep on track with your accountability partners.

This resource is useful for either a group study or personal reflection. Whichever way you approach the subject, you will be challenged to walk on the road of accountability that leads to integrity. Authentic accountability will never happen until we first realize that we belong not only to God but to one another.

To order this book and others, call:

Wesleyan Publishing House
P.O. Box 50434
Indianapolis, IN 46250-0434

**800-4 WESLEY
(800-493-7539)**

Beyond career, possessions, and prestige lies something far more important. Real Meaning in Life!

BK818 $15.99

Reflect for a moment on the life you're living today. Is it balanced? Fulfilling? Meaningful? Or has your bottom-line personality turned your life into a never-ending list of to-do's that leaves you dissatisfied and empty?

Stop letting the momentum of life deprive you of its meaning! *Soul Management* shows you how to transform your dissatisfaction into motivation for finding the fulfillment you desire. This book will help you develop a vision of what God wants your life to be while exploring tough issues like money, time, God's will, and keeping your promises. You can shed life's outer wrappers to arrive at its core: a sense of purpose that will redefine and re-energize your life.

Ideal for personal study or especially for men's groups!

To order this book and others, call:

Wesleyan Publishing House
P.O. Box 50434
Indianapolis, IN

800-4 WESLEY
00-493-7539)